T0096858

RAND

The Accrual Method for Funding Military Retirement

Assessment and Recommended Changes

Richard L. Eisenman, David W. Grissmer, James Hosek, William W. Taylor

Prepared for the
Office of the Secretary of Defense

National Defense Research Institute

The research described in this report was sponsored by the Office of the Secretary of Defense (OSD). The research was conducted in RAND's National Defense Research Institute, a federally funded research and development center supported by the OSD, the Joint Staff, the unified commands, and the defense agencies under Contract DASW01-95-C-0059.

Library of Congress Cataloging-in-Publication Data

The accrual method for funding military retirement : assessment and recommended changes / Richard Eisenman ... [et al.].
     p.   cm.
  "Prepared for the Office of the Secretary of Defense by RAND's National Defense Research Institute."
  "MR-811-OSD."
  Includes bibliographical references (p.).
  ISBN 0-8330-2707-7
  1. Military pensions—United States. 2. United States—Armed Forces—Appointments and retirements. 3. United States—Armed Forces—Appropriations and expenditures. 4. Accrual basis accounting. I. Eisenman, Richard, 1928 - .
  UB373.A23   2001
  353.5 ' 49—dc21
                                         99-11287
                                                 CIP

RAND is a nonprofit institution that helps improve policy and decisionmaking through research and analysis. RAND® is a registered trademark. RAND's publications do not necessarily reflect the opinions or policies of its research sponsors.

Published 2001 by RAND
1700 Main Street, P.O. Box 2138, Santa Monica, CA 90407-2138
1200 South Hayes Street, Arlington, VA 22202-5050
201 North Craig Street, Suite 102, Pittsburgh, PA 15213-1516
RAND URL: http://www.rand.org/
To order RAND documents or to obtain additional information, contact Distribution Services: Telephone: (310) 451-7002; Fax: (310) 451-6915; Internet: order@rand.org

PREFACE

This study examines the operation of the accrual method for funding the military retirement system initiated by Congress in 1984. It replaced the pay-as-you-go method in order to confront Department of Defense (DoD) decisionmakers with the full future costs of their personnel decisions at the time the decisions are made.

The problem with the pay-as-you-go method was that today's decisions affecting future retirement costs would influence DoD budgets only in the distant future; thus, little motivation existed to manage retirement costs efficiently. The accrual method was created to reflect accurately the changing long-term costs of military retirement by changing annual accrual contributions. DoD resource managers would therefore be able to make improved tradeoffs between different types of personnel and between personnel and other categories of expenditures, such as capital equipment and readiness expenditures, because accurate future retirement costs would now be included in the near-term budgets.

This report examines the accrual method from 1985 to 1995 and determines whether the congressional objectives of improved management are being met; identifies those features of the retirement system that inhibit achieving those objectives; makes recommendations for specific changes that will help meet Congress's intent; and assesses the fiscal consequences of such changes. We carried out the research in conjunction with the drawdown of military personnel to aid in projecting the timing and amount of savings in retirement accrual contributions arising from the drawdown. The report contains projections of the military accrual contributions under different drawdown assumptions from 1992 through 1997.

This research was conducted for the Under Secretary for Personnel and Readiness and his predecessors within the Forces and Resources Policy Center of RAND's National Defense Research Institute, a federally funded research and development center sponsored by the Office of the Secretary of Defense, the Joint Staff, the unified commands, and the defense agencies.

CONTENTS

FIGURES

TABLES

SUMMARY

BACKGROUND

Until 1984, the amount appearing in the DoD budget under "military retirement" was the annual payment to retired military personnel or their survivors--equaling approximately $16 billion that year. That amount reflected the number of retirees and the retirement system that resulted from force-management decisions made 20 or more years earlier. Those managing the personnel force in 1984 essentially had no control over these retirement-budget payments. Similarly, force managers in 1984 could make decisions influencing future retirement expenditures without answering for them in their own budgets. Policymakers were concerned that this system could result in increasingly expensive retirement plans, a more senior force, more retirees than justified by force-readiness considerations, and poor decisions involving substitution of civilian and military personnel and between capital and labor investments.

In an attempt to remedy this situation, Congress directed DoD in 1984 to switch to an accrual method for accounting for military retirement in the budget process. This method would replace the current outlays for retirement in the Department of Defense (DoD) budget with an amount that reflected the present value of the estimated cost of future retirement benefits earned by each incoming cohort of personnel. Thus, any decision affecting retirement benefits or the number of military personnel reaching retirement from each cohort would theoretically be reflected in changes in the near-term accrual payment. The Department of the Treasury was assigned responsibility for retirement obligations earned for military service prior to October 1, 1984, and DoD received responsibility for retirement obligations earned for service after October 1, 1984. The Treasury would also make up losses to the system if DoD's future liabilities were underestimated and collect any savings if overestimated.

The accrual method was to provide appropriate incentives to policymakers to make better tradeoffs in defense management and to improve military personnel policies. This purpose is both cited in the congressional documentation and reinforced by the fact that the military retirement fund received no new appropriations. In essence, it is the accounting structure of a trust fund without real funding.

OBJECTIVE

This report examines the operation of the accrual method from FY84 through FY94. It examines the current accrual method to determine the extent to which it provides the desired incentives for improved manpower management. It analyzes the operation of the system since its inception to determine whether it has affected DoD manpower decisions and whether the method has created the conditions necessary for operationalizing effective management incentives. It makes recommendations for changing the method in a way that would strengthen the links between DoD payments and changing retirement liabilities so that service personnel managers would be able to predict accurate accrual payments from policy choices and bear the consequences of their decisions.

THE ACCRUAL METHOD: STRENGTHS AND WEAKNESSES

Our analysis of the current accrual method shows that it has been partially successful in providing incentives for improved defense management, but it has also failed to provide those incentives in several critical areas. The method has provided a mechanism to manage the structuring of retirement benefits better, and it can be credited with an important role in the restructuring of benefits (REDUX) that occurred in 1986. The accrual method will also be an integral part of any future restructuring of retirement benefits. One key to its role in restructuring retirement benefits is that it directly links annual congressional appropriations for retirement to the future level of retirement benefits. The method has also provided improved estimates of the relative costs of active versus reserve retirement benefits, which could improve decisionmaking about the mix of active and reserve forces.

However, the current method fails to provide appropriate incentives to manage the number of individuals retiring from service, to handle

changes in force size, or to provide appropriate incentives to each
service to manage its personnel efficiently. These flaws limit the
method's ability to accomplish its key objectives.

We postulate that four conditions are necessary for the accrual
method to produce improved management incentives.

- DoD accrual payments accurately reflect the changing costs of
  retirement liabilities from year to year and the relative costs
  of retirement liabilities for different types of military
  personnel.
- Budgetary accrual contributions respond accurately and
  reasonably quickly to changed DoD retirement liabilities.
- Policymakers can understand and predict these changes in
  accrual contributions when evaluating personnel options.
- Policymakers bear the consequences of their policy choices
  through fungibility between accrual budgets and other budget
  items.

Five aspects of the current method limit its ability to provide
these incentives. First, the method does not incorporate the effects of
personnel policy changes affecting retirement liabilities accurately or
quickly. The accrual method fails to capture accurately the full
effects of changing manpower policies because it does not incorporate
the key behavioral links between changing pay and retirement benefits
and changing retention behavior. The slow responsiveness results
primarily from the use of a single entry-age normal cohort that fails to
capture the dynamic differences in service-retention behavior among
entry cohorts. Retention patterns used in the age entry-normal cohort
reflect experience from 5 to 15 years ago. While more-recent rates
would be an improvement, a single cohort can never solve the problem of
incorporating the dynamic differences between cohorts. Capturing this
dynamic behavior is particularly important during force drawdowns or
when personnel policies change rapidly. Nowhere does the weakness of
the current method appear more graphically than in a force drawdown,

which substantially reduces retirement liabilities that the current method was unable to incorporate automatically in its estimations.

Second, the annual estimates of unfunded liability, as well as DoD and Treasury contributions over the first 10 years of operation, have been inaccurate. This inaccuracy has resulted from conservative assumptions for pay growth, inflation, and interest rates, in addition to failure to consider the dynamics of the drawdown. These inaccuracies would have little effect if the annual errors were random—sometimes high and sometimes low. However, the annual estimates for unfunded liability have not only been high in each year since the inception of the system, but the overestimates compared to original estimates in 1984 have been substantial, amounting to $333 billion from 1984 to 1994—an average of $30.3 billion per year. The net result of these inaccurate estimates has been a significant increase in the amount of DoD funding to the system compared to the amount required if the estimates had been accurate; annual DoD payments, which amounted to $165 billion between 1984 and 1994, would have been reduced by approximately $30–$40 billion. While inaccurate estimates also caused Treasury payments to be too high, the Treasury gets the difference back through significantly reduced future payments. There is no parallel mechanism to return overpayments to DoD.

Third, no predictable link exists between changing manpower policies and changing annual accrual contributions that personnel planners can use to determine the cost of alternative policies. As a result, personnel planners consider accrual estimates to be exogenous. Part of this problem is caused by the arbitrary and unpredictable changes both in decrement rates and in economic assumptions that have characterized the method. However, most of the problem arises from reliance on a single age-entry normal cohort, rather than utilization of all cohorts, in the estimate of the normal cost percentage.

Fourth, the method does not estimate separate normal cost percentages for each service based on its personnel policies. Because service policies result in different proportions of retirees for entering cohorts, the result is large cross-subsidies of retirement costs across services and effective elimination of service incentives to manage retirement costs. The Army is the most significant loser in the current method.

Fifth, and perhaps most important, the lack of assured fungibility of accrual funds at the service level results in little attention by policymakers to accrual estimates. While history shows that DoD often recovers accrual gains when they are large, such recovery is the result of negotiation between the Office of the Secretary of Defense (OSD), the Office of Management and Budget (OMB), and Congress. Furthermore, recovered funds have not been returned to the services in proportion to services' contributions, but rather allocated by OSD for priority items. Thus, not only are services uncertain whether accrual savings will be fungible, but if they are, OSD will control them. This largely eliminates incentives at the service level for efficient management of retirement obligations.

RECOMMENDATIONS FOR DoD CHANGE

We make the following recommendations to address these problems:

- Improve the quality, timeliness, and accuracy of information available to personnel managers about the consequences of their actions on retirement liabilities by
  - estimating "cohort-specific" normal-cost percentage (NCPs) in the entry-age normal methodology
  - using separate NCPs by service for officers and enlisted personnel
  - introducing a more disciplined and more informed process of setting future values of economic assumptions and military retention rates by
    -- annually evaluating and updating retention and economic assumptions
    -- incorporating prospective changes in retention and pay when such changes are part of overall defense and national policy and conform to other budget guidance
    -- recognizing historical relationships among the internal economic and retention parameters as reflected by consensus in the research community and relationships between the

economic parameters in this method and other macroeconomic
parameters used to formulate national budgets
- changing the composition of the Board of Actuaries to
include representation by economists in the military personnel
research community.

- Make managers bear more directly the consequences of their
policy changes by
  - allocating to DoD rather than Treasury the portion of annual
gains and losses in retirement liabilities attributable to
service after October 1, 1984
  - using separate NCPs by service for officer and enlisted
personnel
  - returning to the services recovered spending authority from
accrual reductions rather than allocating recovered funds at
the OSD level
  - moving to an advance-funded system wherein fungibility is
automatic to each service.

Our research suggests that the following actions should be taken.
First, DoD should adopt a cohort-specific entry-age normal methodology
rather than the single age-entry cohort method now in place. The step
simply requires determination of an accrual contribution for each annual
cohort. The total DoD contribution is then a sum across all cohorts.
This method produces more-accurate and more responsive calculations of
the accrual contribution. Better management normally results from more-
accurate data, and managers who can immediately see the results of their
actions--and carry the responsibility for them--have increased incentive
to make good decisions. **Second**, DoD should receive the gains or losses
in retirement liability attributable to service after October 1, 1984.
This step will allow DoD to accrue any savings--or pay any costs--that
result from its personnel decisions. **Third**, DoD should compute cost
percentages by service for officer and enlisted forces. This action
will make each service responsible for its own portion of the retirement
liability and end cross-subsidies between ranks and services. It will

also enable the services to compute their own liability. **Fourth**, the Board of Actuaries should adopt a more disciplined and more informed process of setting future values of economic assumptions and retention rates. Such a process will produce more-accurate estimates and increase the motivation for responsible personnel decisions. This process would require broadening the membership of the Board of Actuaries to include members with expertise in manpower planning or labor economics. **Fifth**, the method should move to advance funding in order to ensure fungibility at the service level.

While the accrual method has had some identifiably significant positive effects on DoD personnel decisionmaking, it needs change to achieve fully the objectives envisioned by Congress. The management incentives have not been operationalized within the services, and significant changes are required to do so. The Board of Actuaries has recommended some of these changes, and it is congressional inaction that is currently preventing many from being implemented.

ACKNOWLEDGMENTS

We would like to acknowledge the cooperation of the DoD Office of the Actuary in helping us to understand the accrual method and providing data for this report. Bernard Rostker, the RAND program director, and Carl Dahlman, of the Office of the Secretary of Defense, provided both substantive guidance and leadership in turning this research into policy. We also acknowledge John Grady, Kathleen Utgoff, Sam Gutterman, and Caroline Weaver, who served on a RAND-appointed committee to review our work and make recommendations to the Board of Actuaries. Their review and insight are incorporated into this report in several places. We acknowledge the reviews done by John Warner and Michael Hurd that resulted in significant improvements both in substance and exposition.

1. INTRODUCTION

Until 1984, the amount appearing in the Department of Defense (DoD) budget under military retirement was the annual amount paid to current retired military personnel or their survivors. This amount, which totaled about $16 billion in FY84, was unique among military personnel appropriations in that it was insensitive to changes in current manpower or retirement policies. For example, a significant increase today in the size of the armed forces would eventually increase the number of retirees and future retirement obligations; however, these larger expenditures would not show up in the federal budget for some 20 years, and their effect would continue for yet another 40 years. Thus, this system provided little incentive for efficient management of military retirement outlays.

This situation prompted a number of concerns. First, this pay-as-you-go method could result in a too-senior military force that would produce too many retirees and an overly generous retirement system. Tomorrow's decisionmakers would bear the cost of today's decisions. Moreover, underestimating the real cost of current manpower could bias decisions concerning substitution among different types of personnel (civilian versus military) or tradeoffs between capital and labor, making defense too labor-intensive. The bias in these decisions can be large because retirement costs are a significant part of military personnel costs. An indication of the magnitude of retirement costs is that initial accrual estimates made for 1984-1989 show that an amount equal to approximately 48-51 percent of the base active-duty military pay for all personnel would be required to fund future retirement obligations.

Not assigning full and accurate retirement costs to each type of military personnel (officer/enlisted, junior/senior, reserve/active, Army/Air Force/Navy/Marine Corps) can also bias substitutions among these types of personnel. The main reason that retirement costs vary among groups of personnel is that the probability of achieving retirement vesting varies dramatically by group. These varying probabilities would lead to different government contributions to achieve sound actuarial funding for each group. For instance, estimates made in this report show that contributions for enlisted personnel would need to be about 40 percent of pay compared with 66 percent for officers, and contributions for enlisted personnel of each service would range from 39 percent of pay for the Air Force and Army to 32 percent for the Navy and 29 percent for the Marine Corps. Thus, significant bias can occur by not only failing to include the full costs of retirement in personnel decisions, but also by failing to specify accurate costs for each type of service member and service.

AN ACCRUAL ACCOUNTING METHOD FOR FUNDING MILITARY RETIREMENT

In an effort to correct these problems, Congress established in 1984 an accrual accounting method for military retirement. An accrual method attempts to reflect the liability arising from future retirees in current budgets. Public Law 98-94 states that the fund is to cover all retirement liabilities incurred from service after October 1, 1984. The annual accrual charge should "be sufficient to pay for the future retirement benefits for a cohort of new entrants." Congress authorized an age-entry normal system as the basic actuarial mechanism for making DoD contributions to the accrual fund. This mechanism assumes that DoD will contribute a constant percentage of an individual service member's pay annually to the accrual account.

Congress's primary intent in establishing the military accrual method was to provide DoD personnel managers with incentives for more efficient resource-allocation decisions. It intended that the accrual charge accurately estimate future retirement costs for each category of military personnel and provide accurate and rapid budgetary feedback for any policy changes that affected retirement liabilities arising from service after October 1, 1984. For instance, actions moving toward a more junior force structure with fewer individuals reaching retirement should be reflected contemporaneously in changed accrual budgets.

OBJECTIVE OF THE REPORT

The accrual method has been in operation since 1984, and this report examines its operation from FY84 through FY94. Operating from the assumption that management incentives were one of the primary goals for changing the retirement system, this report examines the current accrual method to determine whether it provides the desired incentives for improved manpower management. It analyzes the operation of the method since its inception to determine whether the method has affected DoD manpower decisions and whether DoD contributions have accurately reflected changes in the retirement liability assigned to them. It recommends changing the method to strengthen the links between DoD payments and changing retirement liabilities so that service personnel managers will be accountable for their decisions and manage personnel costs more efficiently.

ORGANIZATION OF THIS REPORT

Section 2 describes the objectives and design of the current accrual method. Section 3 assesses the empirical evidence for the accrual method's affecting personnel decisions and identifies its limitations for providing management incentives. Section 4 spells out our recommended changes, and Section 5 estimates the effect of these changes on accrual payments. Section 6 summarizes conclusions and recommendations. The appendix contains a sample calculation of a normal cost percentage using actual data.

2. THE OBJECTIVES AND DESIGN OF THE MILITARY RETIREMENT ACCRUAL METHOD

OBJECTIVES OF THE CURRENT ACCRUAL METHOD

Congress implemented a new financing mechanism for military retirement in 1984 through Public Law 98—94 (currently Chapter 74, Title 10, U.S. Code).[1] The legislation eliminated "pay-as-you-go" funding for military retirement and replaced it with an accrual accounting procedure. The objective of the law was to "permit the military services to recognize the full costs of manpower decisions made in the current year . . . so the services would manage their forces in different ways and different tradeoffs would occur" [HASC]. This law specifically directed that the budget item for military retirement that was the amount paid out to current retirees be replaced with annual payments into a trust fund such that these payments, plus the accumulated interest, would be sufficient to retire the unfunded liability for current retirees and pay all future retirement obligations.

The legislation sought to make the annual retirement expenditure sensitive to future retirement obligations rather than those already incurred. Presumably, this sensitivity to future obligations would provide incentives for improved management, because personnel policymakers could change future retirement obligations by controlling the number of retirees and their retirement pay, thereby changing the present and future level of payments into the fund. Congress

---

[1]Three primary references are used in this description. They are Chapter 74, Title 10, United States Code, which incorporates the original legislation from Public Law 98—94, together with subsequent modifications, to be referred to subsequently as [Chap 74]; Department of Defense Authorization Act, 1984, Report of the Committee on Armed Services, Report No. 98—107, 98th Congress, House of Representatives, Section 1053, "Accrual Funding for the Military Retirement System," May 11, 1983, to be referred to subsequently as [HASC]; and the annual publications, *Valuation of the Military Retirement System*, that have been issued annually by the Department of Defense, Office of the Actuary, from 1986 through 1996. We refer to these as [VMRS, year of publication].

appropriated no additional money to fund the legislation.[2] Instead, the accounting structure it established suggested that the purpose was improved incentives to manage personnel efficiently, rather than make future retirement obligations more secure.

The key question is the extent to which the structure of the current method has operationalized management incentives. This is partly an empirical question of whether personnel decisions made since the start of the accrual method reflect its influence. We assess this empirical evidence in Section 3. We also specify the operational conditions needed to link accrual contributions to management incentives. To understand whether the current method satisfies these conditions, we first must outline how the current method operates.

OPERATION OF THE MILITARY RETIREMENT FUND

Specifically, the law

- established the DoD Military Retirement Fund to "be used for the accumulation of funds in order to finance on an actuarially sound basis liabilities of the Department of Defense under military retirement and survivor benefit programs"
- moved the obligation for retirement expenditures arising from service before October 1, 1984 (the unfunded liability), from DoD to the Department of the Treasury, and authorized annual Treasury contributions to retire this obligation
- moved payments for current and future retirement liabilities from DoD to Treasury, and replaced the DoD retirement budget with annual accrual payments estimated by the entry-age normal methodology sufficient to fund future retirement and survivor

---

[2]The financing mechanism established by Congress is more accurately called an accrual cost accounting system with no advance funding. The DoD and Treasury "contributions" are essentially costs to their respective departments, but are offset by income to the military retirement "fund." The net effect on the government is to require no new taxes, nor does the system affect the budget deficit or government debt to the public. For additional information, see *Report to the President and Congress on the Status of the Department of Defense Military Retirement Fund*, September 1988, Department of Defense, Retirement Board of Actuaries.

benefits arising from each entering cohort serving after
October 1, 1984

- established a Board of Actuaries appointed by the President to
  make key decisions involving the system, including
  determination of the original unfunded liability and annual
  contributions, and established an Office of the Actuary within
  DoD to implement the system
- specified that any annual gains or losses to the fund be
  accounted separately from the original liability, and that they
  be amortized in accordance with a schedule and methodology
  established by DoD "through an increase or decrease in the
  payments that would otherwise be made to the Fund" by the
  Treasury [Chap 74, 1465(c)(2)—(4)].

Figure 2.1 shows the operation of the current fund. The fund has
three sources of income:

- the accrual payments made by DoD to fund future retirement
  benefits
- the Treasury payments to amortize the original unfunded
  liability
- the interest earned by the assets in the fund.

It has two expenditures: payment of actual benefits and purchase
of special-issue Treasury bonds. All fund transactions are
intragovernmental transfers, except for actual outlays to retirees.
Thus, these latter payments are the only transactions directly affecting
the total federal deficit.

Implementation of the system requires an annual estimate of five
key parameters:

- the current and future accrual payment made by DoD
- the annual current payment and future payments made by Treasury
  to amortize the original unfunded liability
- the annual actuarial gain or loss

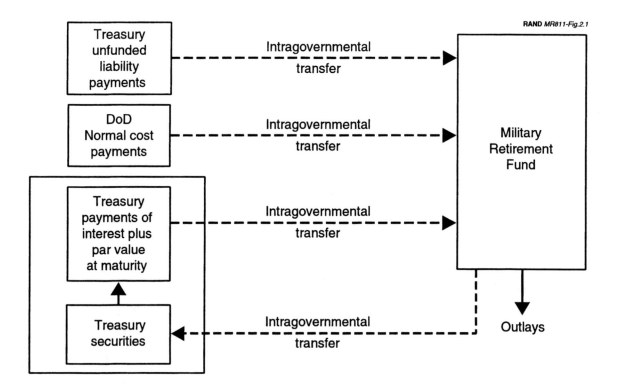

Figure 2.1—Schematic of the Operation of the Military Retirement Fund

- the annual current and future levels of unfunded liability
- the amount of interest in the current and future years earned by the fund.

The DoD Contribution: The Entry-Age Normal Method

The entry-age normal method of funding retirement liabilities assumes that a constant percentage of a service member's military pay is set aside and accumulated over the member's service and that this fund and accrued interest will be just sufficient to pay all future retirement obligations for the service member. This method requires estimation of the constant percentage of pay required to achieve sound funding. This constant percentage is called the normal cost percentage (NCP). Determining the NCP requires three steps:

1. Compute the present value of future retirement benefits for a typical new entrant cohort.

2. Compute the present value of basic military pay for that cohort.

3. Compute the NCP as the ratio of 1 to 2.

Three factors primarily determine the NCP: the structure of retirement benefits, economic assumptions (i.e., the rate and growth of basic pay over time, the cost of living adjustments [COLAs] to pension benefits, and the interest or discount rate used to determine present value), and the percentage of personnel retiring from a cohort.[3]   Below we describe the procedures and assumptions used.

Structure of Retirement Benefits

Retirement plans were redesigned in 1980 and again in 1986, resulting in three distinct military retirement benefit categories called Final Pay (FP), HI-3, and REDUX. A service member falls into one of the categories depending upon his or her date of entry. Each change reduced the retirement benefit. The benefit for each category can be calculated by appropriately modifying the following formula:

$$RET = m(YOS)*(BPay) \tag{1}$$

where

RET	=	Initial Annual Retirement Benefit
m	=	Retirement Multiplier
YOS	=	Years of Service, and
BPay	=	Pay Parameter (base pay in Table 2.2)

---

[3]Our description and calculations will include only active-duty personnel receiving normal retirement benefits. This specifically excludes reserve-force personnel and active-duty personnel receiving disability retirement benefits or any survivor benefits. The personnel and benefits included in our calculations account for over 80 percent of retirement liabilities. Generally, the disability and survivor benefits are small compared with the normal benefits, and create only a small bias in the NCP calculations. In 1986, the reserve-force contributions were separated from active contributions and calculated independently; they constitute about 10—15 percent of total contributions. Although these aspects of the Military Retirement System are important, the major points in our argument can be made using active-duty personnel receiving normal benefits. Of course, this simplifies our calculations and description enormously compared with the DoD actuarial models.

- 9 -

Table 2.1

Methods for Computing Military Retirement

Category	Applies to those entering service:	Formula
FP	Prior to Sep. 8, 1980	2.5% × YOS × Final base pay
HI-3	Between Sep. 8, 1980, and Aug. 1, 1986	2.5% x YOS × Average of highest three years of base pay
REDUX	After Aug. 1, 1986	2.5% × YOS - (1% for each year under 30) × Average of highest three years of base pay[a]

[a]The 1-percent-per-year offset is eliminated when a retiree reaches age 62.

The computation method for each of the three categories appears in Table 2.1.

Under this system, a retiree in the FP category with 20 years of service receives 50 percent of final base pay, and one with 30 years of service receives 75 percent. A HI-3 20-year retiree would receive 50 percent of the average of the highest three years of base pay, and a REDUX retiree with 20 years of service would receive 40 percent (30 years - 20 years = 10 years × 1 percent = 10 percent reduction) and 75 percent at 30 years of service.

The REDUX method also calculates COLAs differently than the previous two methods. The annual adjustment in benefits for both the FP and HI-3 categories is equal to the full COLA, which is currently linked to the annual change in the Consumer Price Index (CPI). The annual adjustment for the REDUX group is obtained by subtracting 1 percent from the full COLA. However, a one-time catch-up payment is applied when its members reach age 62, although the reduced annual adjustments continue thereafter.

Economic Assumptions

The key economic assumptions required to make the necessary projections are

- the annual growth rate for military basic pay
- the annual interest rate used to compute future interest on plan assets and used for discounting present values
- the annual COLA for retirement pensions (also assumed to be the inflation rate).

The actuaries use different sets of values for the near- and long-term projections. Near-term projections (usually five years) typically use values closer to current levels. For the longer term, steady-state values are used for all years. The DoD Retirement Board of Actuaries is responsible for setting these values so that they are "based on actuarial assumptions that are reasonable in the aggregate." The board has made several revisions of assumptions, partly in response to the large actuarial gains registered by the system. Table 2.2 shows the original economic assumptions and the changes made since 1984.[4]

The calculation of liabilities also requires that average military pay be specified by years of service. This means computing an average across different grade distributions in each year of service (YOS). The expected relative level of pay by years of service has been stable in recent years, so the Actuary uses an average distribution based on 1981–1984 profiles.

Table 2.2

Long-Term Values Used in Economic Assumptions

Assumptions	FY85–88	FY89–91	FY91–94	FY94+
Military Pay	6.2	5.75	5.5	4.5
Interest Rate	6.6	7.0	7.5	6.75
COLA	5.0	5.0	5.0	4.0

SOURCE: DoD, Office of the Actuary, *Valuation of the Military Retirement System* (VMRS) (1986-1996).

---

[4]The formulas, methods, and assumptions for making the present value and other calculations are given in annual reports (1984-1994) on the fund, VMRS, published by the Office of the Actuary. These reports are our primary source of data for analyzing the operation of the system.

Percentage of Personnel Retiring (Decrement Rate)

An important part of the liability calculation involves determining how many service members will achieve vesting (presently reached at 20 years of service), how many vested members will depart before 30 years, and how long the retirement benefits will continue. The most important decrement rates involve the retention rates of personnel to retirement eligibility at 20 years of service, which represent the proportion of a cohort retiring. Retention rates after retirement eligibility determine the timing of retirement and the beginning and level of retirement payments. Mortality experience then dictates the longevity of payments.

The actuary develops "typical" retention rates for a current incoming cohort by drawing on historical data. The retention profile developed by the actuary combines longitudinal retention experience with recent cross-sectional experience.[5] This composite retention profile began with the retention profiles of cohorts entering in 1978–1980. Their retention experience is tracked to the most recently available reporting period, e.g., September 30, 1988. Averaging across these cohorts gives a longitudinal profile for the first nine years of service (1980-1981,..., 1988-1989). The profile is completed by appending the most recent cross-sectional rates for years of service 10 to 30.

Mortality rates from standard actuarial tables complete the computation of retirement liabilities. Once the continuation rates have been estimated, they are used to synthesize a typical new-entry cohort (actually cohorts--one for officers, one for enlistees) by taking a nominal entry group and applying the continuation rates to determine the number remaining on active duty in each subsequent year.

Estimating the Normal Cost Percentage: Solving the Problem of Three Benefit Groups

Using the assumptions stated above, we can compute the present value of both retirement liabilities and total pay for a "typical" new entering cohort. However, a problem remains in deciding how to treat benefit groups who entered under different retirement systems. There is

---

[5]The Actuary's annual report does not describe the exact methods used to develop these retention rates. The methodology described here resulted from conversations with the DoD Actuary.

no "typical" retirement benefit but rather three different benefits depending on when individuals entered the military.

One approach would be to assume that all new cohorts would be eligible only for REDUX benefits, and incorporate the REDUX benefit into the "typical" cohort. This approach would be partly supported by the legislative mandate that required DoD funding "sufficient to fund a typical new entering cohort." However, the legislation also specifies that "all retirement benefits resulting from service performed on or after October 1, 1984" should be DoD's liability. Because a large number of current and future retirees with service after that date will not fall in the REDUX retirement-benefit category, some modification is required to fulfill this mandate. It is instructive to examine how this problem of "atypical" benefit cohorts was solved, because it can serve as a model for unraveling the problem of "atypical" *retention* behavior in cohorts as well.

The problem was solved by resorting to multiple cohorts. The procedure involves running the same synthetic cohort through separate projection computations using each of the three distinct benefit categories to obtain distinct NCPs for each of the benefit groups. The three computations use identical decrement rates and economic assumptions. In solving this problem, the actuaries realized that the DoD accrual contributions should recognize actual historical cohorts with different benefit structures.

However, in the assumption of similar economic and retention rates for the three cohorts, these parameters do not change for cohorts entering in different eras. As Figure 2.2 shows, enlisted cohorts entering prior to 1980 (FP) had lower retention rates than the other cohorts. Likewise, pay growth and economic assumptions for these cohorts differed from more recent cohorts. So, an extension of this methodology developed by the actuary would have incorporated not only the different historical benefit structure but also the different historic retention behavior and economic assumptions corresponding to each benefit structure. Such an approach--a pure cohort accounting framework--is one we later recommend.

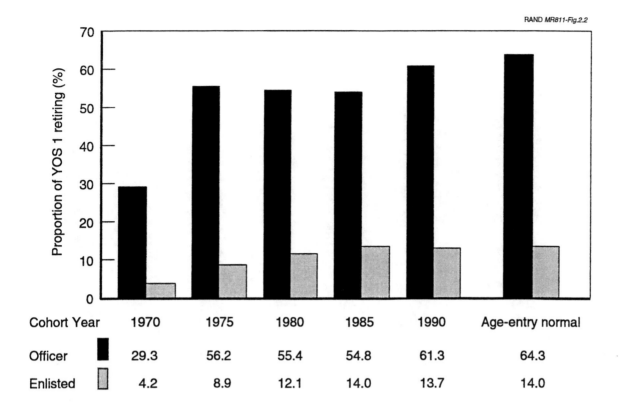

SOURCE: Annual personnel counts and continuation-rate data provided by the Defense Manpower Data Center.

Figure 2.2--Probability of Retirement for Entering Cohorts

Using the same continuation assumptions for each cohort, the actuary generates three NCPs corresponding to a pre-1980 cohort, a HI-3 cohort, and a REDUX cohort. According to the actuary, the NCP for the FY86 FP active-duty group is 55.1 percent, while HI-3 is 48.2 percent and REDUX is 40.3 percent. In 1994, the corresponding numbers are 39.3, 35.0, and 29.7. Once the actuary develops separate NCPs by benefit cohort, an overall aggregate NCP must be calculated. Weighting the three NCPs according to the proportion of the current payroll paid by each benefit group achieves this. Figure 2.3 shows the original estimated NCP compared with actual and projected values for 1985–1994.

The annual accrual payment will then be the product of the aggregate NCP and the total annual payroll. Figure 2.4 shows the estimated and actual DoD accrual contributions from 1986 to 1995. We will identify the reasons for the differences in projected and actual

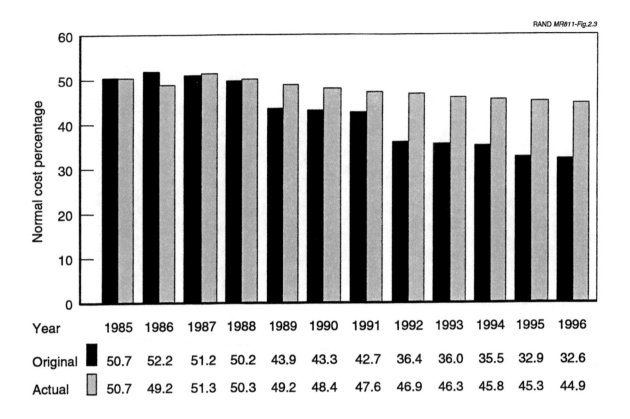

Year	1985	1986	1987	1988	1989	1990	1991	1992	1993	1994	1995	1996
Original	50.7	52.2	51.2	50.2	43.9	43.3	42.7	36.4	36.0	35.5	32.9	32.6
Actual	50.7	49.2	51.3	50.3	49.2	48.4	47.6	46.9	46.3	45.8	45.3	44.9

SOURCE: VMRS (1986-1996).

Figure 2.3--Active Duty Normal Cost Percentage

payments. The appendix contains a sample computation for an NCP using actual data.

The Treasury Payment and Amortization of Gains and Losses

Each year an amortization schedule is established to retire the unfunded liability through payments to the Treasury. The Treasury payment was initially determined by estimating the constant annual percentage of military pay necessary to amortize the unfunded liability over 60 years. This figure was determined through evolution of a model that estimated retirement liabilities, DoD contributions, and investment contributions over those years. The model was run for personnel who entered military service before October 1, 1984, and it estimated that

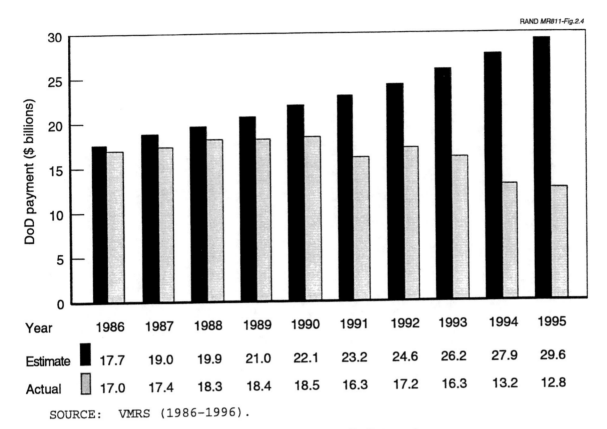

Year	1986	1987	1988	1989	1990	1991	1992	1993	1994	1995
Estimate	17.7	19.0	19.9	21.0	22.1	23.2	24.6	26.2	27.9	29.6
Actual	17.0	17.4	18.3	18.4	18.5	16.3	17.2	16.3	13.2	12.8

SOURCE: VMRS (1986-1996).

Figure 2.4--DoD Accrual Payments

annual payments of approximately 33 percent[6] of military pay were required to amortize the liability over this period.

The legislation requires that any changes in unfunded liability be accounted for separately from the original liability and that they be used to reduce Treasury payments and be amortized in accordance with a schedule and methodology established by the board. The actuaries currently use a 30-year amortization schedule.

Some problems in the current method arise from the basic contradiction in the legislation in stating that *"DoD should pay for all obligations for service after October 1, 1984,"* but that *"Treasury should receive all gains or losses to the system."* Both objectives cannot be met, because annual gains or losses to the system that will go to Treasury will contain liabilities arising for service after 1984 that

---

[6]The payments are actually one-third of the second preceding year's basic payroll because it is the most recent data available at the time of the payment.

DoD should pay for. For instance, a change in the assumptions about COLAs for military retirement pensions in 1990 would affect those who retired both before and after October 1, 1984. For those who retired afterward, a portion of their retirement liability was paid by DoD accrual contributions since October 1, 1984. Because legislation holds DoD responsible for all retirement obligations due to service after October 1, 1984, one could argue that it should receive (or pay) for the latter changes in unfunded liability. However, the system has been implemented according to the latter provision--that Treasury receives all gains and losses to the system, even those arising from service after FY84.

If these gains were small, it would be immaterial who receives them. However, these annual gains were substantial during 1985-1994, as indicated in Figure 2.5, which shows that the unfunded liabilities for the following year have always been overestimated by anywhere from $5

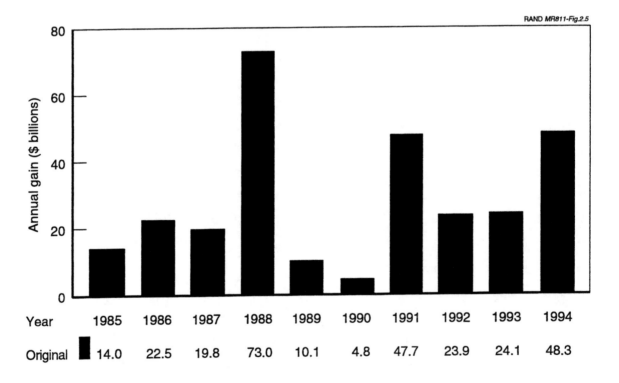

SOURCE: VMRS (1986-1996).

Figure 2.5--Actuarial Gains (Annual Differences in the Estimated Unfunded Liability and Actual Unfunded Liability)

billion to $73 billion. These changes in unfunded liabilities reduce
Treasury payments, and Figure 2.6 compares the actual payment with the
original schedule of unfunded liability payments. The reduction in
Treasury payments in 1994 alone was $13.3 billion, and cumulatively
since inception the Treasury payments have been reduced by $61.2
billion. This reduction in unfunded liability to date also reduces
future Treasury payments significantly over the next 30 years from the
original schedule. We argue that DoD should receive a share of these
gains.

Unfunded Liability: The Role of the Treasury

The unfunded liability arising from service prior to October 1,
1984, was estimated at $528.7 billion--the amount estimated by the
actuaries as needing to be available, together with accrued interest, to
fund all future retirement obligations arising from service before
October 1, 1984. The legislation made the original unfunded liability

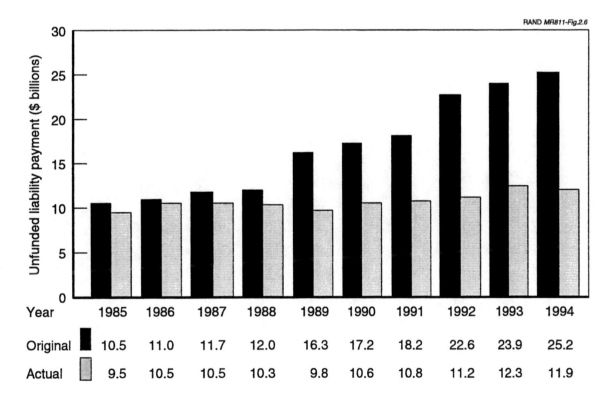

SOURCE: VMRS (1986-1996).

Figure 2.6--Comparison of Actual to Scheduled Treasury Payments

the responsibility of the General Fund of the Treasury, and the Board of Actuaries later determined that it should be amortized in 60 annual payments.

The original unfunded liability as of October 1, 1984, was calculated by assuming no new entrants to military service and

- calculating the present value of all future retirement benefits for those who are currently retired and those who were currently in active or reserve service as of October 1, 1984. This amount was estimated at $692 billion.
- calculating the present value of future DoD contributions (method described below) and interest earned on these contributions from those who were currently in the service. This amount was estimated at $163 billion.
- taking the difference between these two quantities to obtain the original unfunded liability—$529 billion.

An annual recomputation of the unfunded liability uses the same methods (except that fund assets are added as they build up), but uses the force in existence at the end of each fiscal year.

Figure 2.7 compares the estimates of the scheduled annual unfunded liability from 1984 to 1994 that were made in 1984 to the actual estimates made in each year. These data show that the unfunded liability in 1994 has been reduced by $333 billion from original actuary estimates of expected unfunded liabilities in 1984. This annual calculation of unfunded liability may differ from the original amortization schedule for three reasons. First, retirement-benefit formulas may change from those assumed in the original amortization schedule. Second, gain and loss experience (numbers receiving or projected to receive benefits) may differ from that originally assumed. Third, various actuarial assumptions such as military pay growth, inflation rate, and interest rate may also change. A significant cause of the unscheduled reduction in unfunded liability is conservative economic assumptions made by the actuaries that did not materialize and the failure to incorporate the drawdown into estimates.

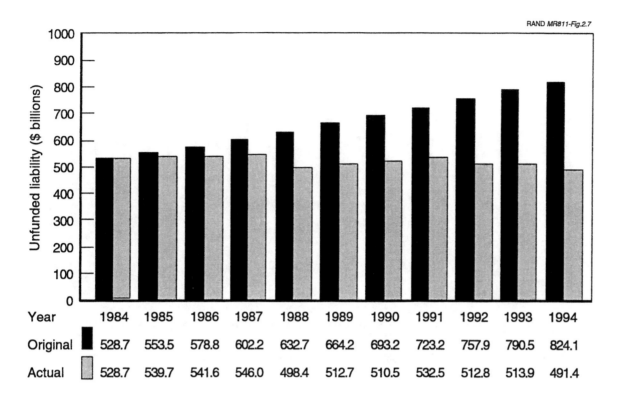

SOURCE: VMRS (1986-1996).

Figure 2.7--Comparison of Estimates of Unfunded Liability (1984 and Annual)

Accumulated Fund Assets

The fund accumulates assets from DoD accrual payments, Treasury payments, and earned interest, and it is reduced by annual retirement obligations. Fund assets are invested in special-issue Treasury obligations that mirror a security issued to the public. Interest rates parallel those paid for the public issue securities. Figure 2.8 shows the accumulated fund assets from 1985-1994.

SUMMARY

This section has described the actuarial methods used in the Military Retirement System and a history of fund flows, economic assumptions, and different retirement-benefit structures. In the next section, we examine the operation of the system since its inception to answer several key questions:

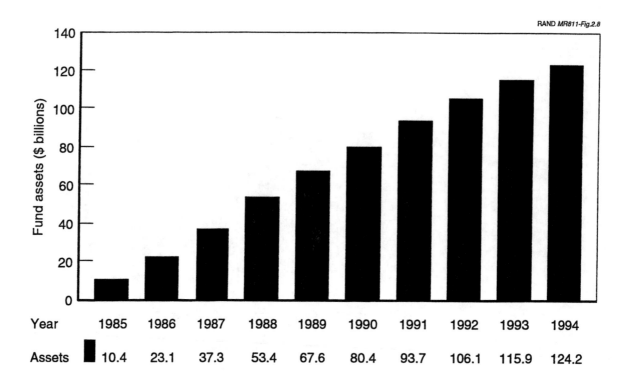

SOURCE: VMRS (1986-1996).

Figure 2.8--Actual Fund Assets

- Which personnel decisions have been affected by the accrual method?

- How does the current method create the conditions necessary for establishing incentives for more-efficient personnel management?

- How do DoD payments reflect the changing retirement liabilities due to service after October 1, 1994, and thus the extent to which DoD payments have been higher or lower than required?

- What is the cause of the large actuarial gains that have significantly reduced Treasury--but not DoD--payments?

- How accurate are the economic assumptions used by the actuaries in the first 10 years of the system?

- How does the method take into account force drawdowns and expansions?

3. MANAGEMENT INCENTIVES IN THE CURRENT SYSTEM

NECESSARY CONDITIONS FOR CREATING MANAGEMENT INCENTIVES IN AN ACCRUAL METHOD

The primary reason underlying congressional direction to adopt an accrual method was to provide DoD incentives for more efficient personnel management. Making the effect of long-term liabilities apparent in near-term budgets has the potential to provide policymakers a real incentive to manage efficiently and to make better tradeoff decisions. However, whether accrual estimates actually create appropriate management incentives in decision situations depends on several factors concerning their accuracy, timeliness, and predictability, and whether the accrual payments are included in discretionary spending. We postulate that four conditions are necessary for the accrual method to produce management incentives:

- DoD accrual payments must accurately reflect the changing costs of retirement liabilities from year to year and the relative costs of retirement liabilities for different types of military personnel.
- Budgetary accrual contributions must respond accurately and reasonably quickly to changed DoD retirement liabilities.
- Policymakers must themselves understand and predict these changes in accrual contributions when evaluating personnel options.
- Policymakers must bear the consequences of their policy choices through fungibility between accrual budgets and other budget items.

We see two ways to assess whether the current method is creating the desired management incentives. The first is to look for empirical evidence that personnel policy decisions have been affected by accrual estimates. The second is to assess how well the current method creates the above conditions.

EMPIRICAL EVIDENCE FOR THE EXISTENCE OF MANAGEMENT INCENTIVES

If accrual contributions are providing management incentives, they should affect manpower and personnel decisions. The presence of accrual estimates might affect several types of decisions in DoD. First, accrual estimates might be used when evaluating the costs of alternative retirement plans. Significant changes have been made in the value of military retirement, and accrual estimates might play an important role in evaluating these alternatives. Secondly, accrual estimates can be used when evaluating the future costs of alternative personnel policies. Service personnel managers annually generate a five-year plan for managing personnel after evaluating several alternatives. Accrual estimates might be used and influence the choices among alternative plans. Issues such as the experience mix of the force would figure in and could also be influenced by accrual estimates. Finally, accrual estimates might be used when evaluating the relative costs of different types of personnel or when assessing tradeoffs among personnel, readiness, and capital expenditures.

The Role of the Accrual Method in Changing Levels of Retirement Benefits

Today's decisionmakers can affect retirement liabilities in two primary ways: they can change the structure of the retirement benefit or alter the number of people who receive it. Only high-level commissions or special task groups change the structure of military retirement benefits; therefore, changes are easier to track than are decisions affecting those receiving benefits.

Efforts to change the military retirement system before the initiation of the accrual method were largely unsuccessful.[1] However, once the accrual system was initiated, it played a central role in the process of changing the structure of military retirement benefits from HI-3 to REDUX in 1986.[2] The normal cost percentage generated in the

_____

[1]President Carter appointed a Presidential Commission to study military pension reform. The recommendations of this commission were generally not implemented, although a change was made in the retirement structure in 1980 from use of the "high one (HI-1)" to "high three (HI-3)" as the basis for computing the retirement benefit.

[2]The Fifth Quadrennial Review of Military Compensation in 1984 studied military pension reform for two years and recommended various

process of accrual estimates provided more visibility to the actual costs of military retirement and enabled easier comparison with private sector systems. This visibility was partly responsible for the congressional initiative to reduce military retirement payments, but more importantly it provided a direct mechanism for Congress to mandate lower benefits. Congress effected a change in the benefit level simply by authorizing a lower budgetary amount for accrual than the projected levels necessary to fund retirement with existing benefits.

In the process of determining the level of benefits that could meet the new accrual budget amounts, the actuaries (and their algorithms) played a central role by working closely with personnel planners to provide estimates of accrual contributions under alternative retirement benefit structures. This illustrates what is required in an accrual method to create management incentives. In this case, personnel planners could see a clear connection between changing benefit structure and changing accrual contributions; they could evaluate various policy options and make decisions through fairly straightforward estimation using the accrual algorithm.

Although one can argue whether the changes in retirement structure represented an improvement in personnel management, no one doubts that the changes could not have been accomplished if the accrual method had not been in place, and that the outcome and policy eventually adopted were shaped by the accrual process. This process provides analysts and policymakers contemplating future retirement benefit changes with a legacy of both precedent and methodology for calculating the effects of changed benefits on DoD contributions, and they would be likely to use such methods in evaluating future changes.

The Role of the Accrual Method in Changing Projected Beneficiaries

The number of beneficiaries can be changed through compensation, promotion, and separation policies or through longer-term decisions regarding force size. These policies are jointly set by Congress,

---

changes. Their work partially formed the basis for the eventual adoption of the REDUX system.

through such mechanisms as end-strength constraints, and DOPMA; the policies set constraints on the number of personnel in senior grades. However, many of these decisions are less visible, and thus the influence of accrual estimates is more difficult to document.[3]

The Role of the Accrual Method in Managing Policies Affecting Personnel Flows

Currently, only a weak link exists between accrual contributions and the year-to-year personnel planning process that determines the number of retirees. Accrual costs in DoD are determined by the product of the current force payroll in a given year and the NCP. The accrual payment is affected directly and immediately by changes in payroll caused by shifts in experience mix and the level of compensation, but the NCP is almost immune to annual changes in personnel plans. Thus, planners generally regard the NCP as exogenous to the personnel planning process.

For instance, if personnel planners were to tighten permanently pre-retirement tenure rules to restrict the number reaching retirement and thereby raise accession levels to keep force size constant, lower present and future payrolls would result and should trigger a lower NCP. Under present methods used by the actuaries, this policy action would lower the payroll in the following year, thereby lowering DoD contributions. However, it would not be reflected in payroll projections for future years nor would it affect the current NCP until years later. The reason is that the projections of future-force structure and the cohort calculations leading to the NCP use continuation rates from 5-15 years ago. Thus, any current change in continuation rates would not be fully reflected for 15 years.

To the extent that personnel managers use the projected payrolls and NCPs given in actuarial reports as the basis for future accrual costs, the costs will not reflect recent policy changes. Service managers can produce relatively easily future payrolls that reflect these recent policy changes based on their own data; they therefore

---

[3]For descriptions of officer and enlisted management, see, for example, Thie and Brown, 1994; Kirby and Thie, 1996.

could compute better estimates of future payroll costs than the actuary, and could fully expect these estimates to be close to what the actuary would use in each future year. However, whether personnel managers make accurate calculations of payroll is unclear, because they largely do not understand how the accrual method works. However, NCPs certainly would not change in response to this policy, and certainly the change in NCP far outweighs the effect of changing payroll for many policy situations. A significant part of the incentive for implementing these policies, therefore, is lost.

Furthermore, another source of bias in accrual estimates hampers accurate evaluation of policies affecting personnel flows. The actuarial methods have no links built into the models that connect future pay raises or changing retirement benefits to assumed future retention rates. Large pay raises would raise service retention rates and the proportion of cohorts retiring, while changes to a REDUX system would lower retention rates prior to 20 years of service and raise them afterward. Research data is available to compute such estimates, which could be used to modify future retention rates for cohorts under different retirement plans and for different levels of pay raises.[4]

Failure to include lower retention rates from the REDUX system in future retention estimates biases DoD payments upward. DoD is paying more than necessary because the future proportion of cohorts retiring will be smaller due to declining benefits. Failure to capture the effects of real pay increases has created bias in the opposite direction because the actuarial assumptions to date have assumed larger than actual real pay increases. The net effect of not linking retention, military pay, and retirement benefits is that the full effects of policy changes made by the services are not captured in future accrual estimates, therefore removing part of the incentive for better management.

Finally, perhaps the main problem with creating appropriate incentives is the lack of service-specific NCPs for officer and enlisted personnel. Figure 3.1 shows an estimate of the proportion of officer

---

[4]See for instance, Asch and Warner, 1994a; Asch and Warner, 1994b.

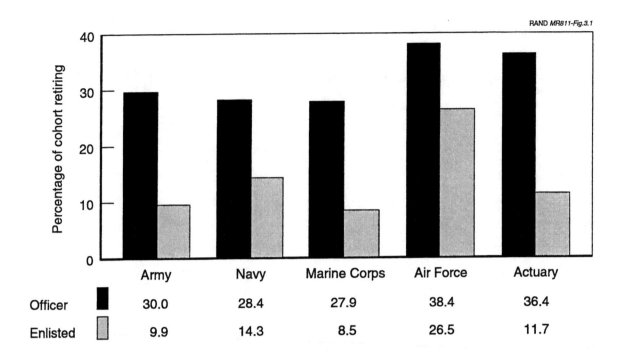

RAND *MR811-Fig.3.1*

	Army	Navy	Marine Corps	Air Force	Actuary
Officer ■	30.0	28.4	27.9	38.4	36.4
Enlisted ▨	9.9	14.3	8.5	26.5	11.7

Figure 3.1--Comparing Actuary and RAND Estimates of the Proportion of an Entering Cohort Reaching Retirement

and enlisted cohorts retiring using pre-drawdown, pre-Desert Storm continuation rates (1987-1989). The data show marked differences in these proportions that would lead to significantly different NCPs for each service. Unfortunately, the current accrual method does not incorporate separate service NCPs but rather generates a DoD-wide NCP that is applied to each service when determining its accrual payment. The current method provides significant subsidies to the Air Force and significantly penalizes the Army and Marine Corps. This system removes much of the incentive for the services to manage personnel flows efficiently because they do not feel the full effect of their policies. The current method provides incentives to the Air Force for a more-senior force because other services subsidize Air Force retirement. The Army is the significant loser in the present arrangement.[5]

---

[5]See Hix and Taylor, 1997, for discussions of the effects on Army budgets and incentives from the current accrual method.

The Role of the Accrual Method in Managing Policies Affecting Force Size and Mix

When the accrual method was implemented in 1984--prior to the dramatic changes in world conditions--the primary personnel policy issues were service seniority, level of compensation and retirement benefits, quality of recruits, and mix of active versus reserve force. Significant changes in force size, either higher or lower, received little consideration. However, the military has been involved in significant post-Cold War force reductions since 1992 and a significant shift from active to reserve forces. In addition, today's smaller force size makes a substantial increase in force size possible if certain threats materialize simultaneously. Examining how the accrual method is linked to force size and active/reserve mix issues is critical.

When the accrual method was initiated, a common NCP was estimated for both active and reserve forces. This procedure introduced significant bias in substitution decisions because reserve retirement costs as estimated by accrual techniques are significantly lower than active costs. In 1987, the system was changed to incorporate separate NCPs for active and reserve forces. Reserve NCPs since 1990 have been less than one-third the size of active-force NCPs; in 1990, the active-force NCP was 43.2, and the reserve NCP was 13.3. This separation of active and reserve NCPs provides improved cost estimates for substitution decisions involving active/reserve forces.

However, the current accrual method cannot respond to those personnel policies that are necessary to reduce or increase force size and therefore cannot incorporate their effects. Reductions in force size during the drawdown have been accomplished through large voluntary separation offers, early-retirement programs, and reduction in accession levels.[6] These programs sharply reduced the numbers of current service personnel between 7 and 19 years of service who will reach retirement eligibility at 20 years of service. This dynamic process should result

---

[6]For a more complete explanation of the drawdown strategy and voluntary-separation offers, see Grissmer, David, Richard Eisenman, and William Taylor, *Defense Downsizing: An Evaluation of Alternative Voluntary Separation Payments to Military Personnel*, MR-171-OSD/A, Santa Monica, Calif.: RAND, 1995.

in reduced accrual contributions through adjustments in the NCP as long as the affected cohorts remain in the service. However, the age-entry normal cohort, which uses continuation rates delayed by 5-15 years, will not incorporate this phenomenon soon enough to provide incentives for these separations. The net result is that DoD will spend billions of dollars to fund separation offers that will reduce the present value of future retirement liabilities even more, but the NCPs will remain essentially unchanged.

To provide management incentives in such force reductions, the accrual payments should immediately reflect lower retirement liabilities, and those reductions should be used to offset the up-front expense of paying the separation costs. Estimates for one Army drawdown plan for enlisted personnel show that the reduction in the present value of retirement liabilities--$3.5 billion--exceeds the cost of separation offers by about 40 percent (Grissmer et al., 1995). However, no mechanism exists in the current accrual method to reflect immediately these reductions in liabilities.

In sum, evidence indicates that the present accrual method has affected decisions about the structure of retirement benefits but not decisions regarding the number of recipients, either through personnel policies or decisions to alter the size of the force.

LIMITATIONS IN THE CURRENT SYSTEM FOR PROVIDING INCENTIVES

Several aspects of the current method keep it from providing incentives for improved management.

The procedure for estimating the retirement liability for each service and DoD results in a biased estimate that in turn biases the accrual contribution. But even if the changes in retirement liability were accurately estimated, the current method often does not incorporate the effects of policy changes quickly and automatically into changed accrual contributions.

Planners cannot currently readily estimate the different accrual contributions resulting from different manpower and personnel plans. In addition, service decisionmakers do not bear the full consequences of their policies because normal cost percentages are not estimated separately by service and officer/enlisted personnel. Nor is the fungibility of accrual funds automatic; it is governed in each instance through negotiations between DoD, OMB, and Congress. Thus, decisionmakers cannot plan for use of savings--but neither are they required to reduce funding in cases of accrual increases.

Biased Estimation of DoD and Service Retirement Liabilities

Management incentives and better decisions can only occur when estimates of retirement liabilities attributable to DoD and the associated annual payments are accurate. DoD is particularly vulnerable to inaccurate projected payments because the gains and losses go to Treasury, not to DoD; gains have been registered each year (see Figure 2.5), with none going to reduce DoD payments.

Four factors currently bias the calculation of DoD and service retirement liabilities:

- conservative assumptions
- use of a single cohort to replace each actual DoD cohort
- failure to calculate separate NCPs by service
- return to the Treasury of gains due to post-FY84 liabilities.

Conservative Assumptions

An accrual method whose sole purpose is providing sufficient funds to pay obligations inherently tends toward conservative assumptions, because the penalties for insufficient funds are much greater than those for excess funds. Such conservative tendencies may be countered in the private sector by incentives to optimize profits. Conservative assumptions may be justified for accrual methods with advance funding in which retirement payments depend on adequate funding; however, they are difficult to justify in a system without advance funding in which management incentives are the prime reason for such a fund. An accrual method meant to provide incentives with no advance funding operates best when assumptions are realistic and retirement liabilities and accrual contributions are estimated accurately.

Conservative assumptions to date regarding pay growth, COLAs, and interest have resulted in significantly higher estimates of unfunded liability and DoD accrual contributions than would have occurred with

accurate assumptions. Figures 3.2, 3.3, and 3.4 compare the actuarial
assumptions for military pay growth, interest, and COLAs with actual
values. Forecasted military pay growth and COLAs have been
significantly higher than experienced, while interest has been much
lower than actual. The directional effect of the error in each factor
is to increase military retirement liabilities for both the Treasury and
DoD, and to have increased the payments into the fund by Treasury and
DoD over what accurate assumptions would have required.

Inaccurate assumptions lead to inaccurate accrual payments. Each
year calculations are made of the actuarial gain or loss from inaccurate
assumptions, and these gains or losses are amortized in an account
currently used to adjust only the Treasury payment. Figure 3.5 shows
the gains attributable to inaccuracies in two assumption categories.
Gains from interest inaccuracy have been the smallest, but have always
been positive and range from zero to a few billion dollars a year.

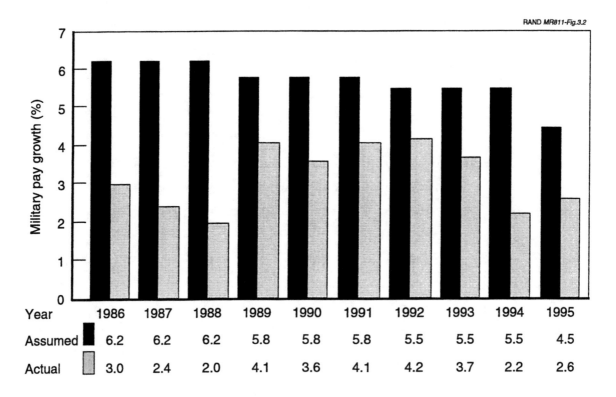

SOURCE: VMRS (1986-1996).

Figure 3.2--Comparison of Assumed and Actual Military Pay Growth

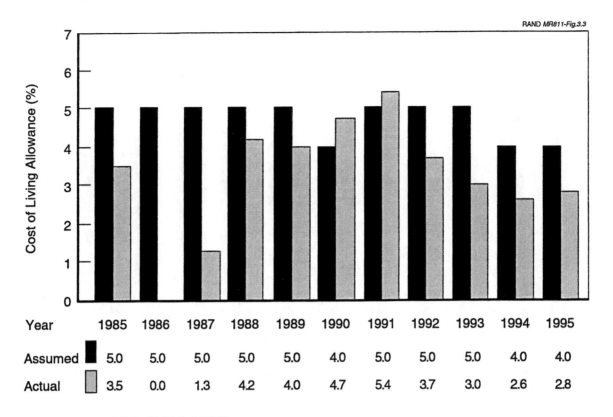

Year	1985	1986	1987	1988	1989	1990	1991	1992	1993	1994	1995
Assumed ■	5.0	5.0	5.0	5.0	5.0	4.0	5.0	5.0	5.0	4.0	4.0
Actual ▓	3.5	0.0	1.3	4.2	4.0	4.7	5.4	3.7	3.0	2.6	2.8

SOURCE: VMRS (1986-1996).
NOTE: No actual values exist for 1986.

Figure 3.3--Comparison of Assumed and Actual COLA

Gains due to inaccuracy in COLAs and military pay growth are combined
and constitute the largest source of gains, ranging from a few billion
dollars to almost $25 billion per year.

The conservative assumptions since FY84 have led to much higher DoD
payments than would have been scheduled had more accurate assumptions
been made, and these gains have reduced future Treasury--not DoD--
payments. The reduction in Treasury payments in 1994 alone was $13.7
billion, and cumulatively since inception Treasury payments have been
reduced by $59.2 billion. This reduction in unfunded liability has also
reduced future Treasury payments significantly over the next 30 years
from the original schedule. Part of these Treasury reductions should go
to lowering the DoD payment if "DoD is responsible for all liabilities
for service after October 1, 1984" [Chap 74].

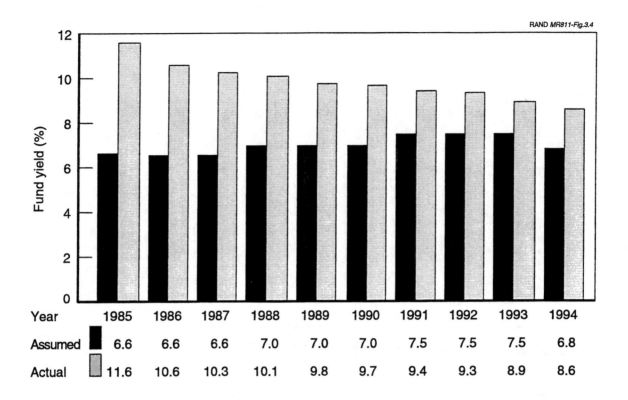

RAND MR811-Fig.3.4

Year	1985	1986	1987	1988	1989	1990	1991	1992	1993	1994
Assumed ■	6.6	6.6	6.6	7.0	7.0	7.0	7.5	7.5	7.5	6.8
Actual ▨	11.6	10.6	10.3	10.1	9.8	9.7	9.4	9.3	8.9	8.6

SOURCE: VMRS (1986–1996).

**Figure 3.4—Comparison of Assumed and
Actual Fund Yield**

Figure 3.6 shows the reaction of the Board of Actuaries, which has
responded to large gains by attempting to make more realistic
assumptions. Each time assumptions change, an additional gain is
registered. The impact of the changes in assumptions in FY88, FY91, and
FY94 are registered as gains of $54, $41, and $23 billion respectively—
all of which eventually returns to Treasury in the form of lower future
payments.

These gains and losses are important only to the extent that they
do not approximately balance out annually. If they merely reflect the
normal random errors in assumptions, then the amortization accounts will
not greatly affect the accrual payments, because contributions over a
number of years will offset them. However, errors that result from
consistently conservative assumptions and from drawdown have not been
random.

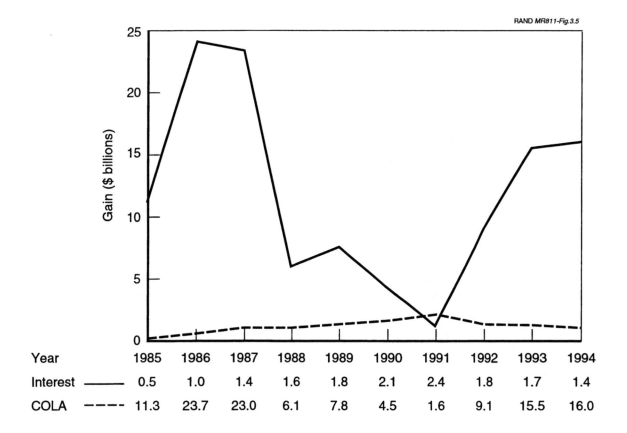

Year	1985	1986	1987	1988	1989	1990	1991	1992	1993	1994
Interest ———	0.5	1.0	1.4	1.6	1.8	2.1	2.4	1.8	1.7	1.4
COLA - - - -	11.3	23.7	23.0	6.1	7.8	4.5	1.6	9.1	15.5	16.0

SOURCE: VMRS (1986-1996).

Figure 3.5--Source of Annual Gains

Use of a Single Cohort

A significant variance also exists in service continuation rates. Figures 3.7 and 3.8 compare actual cumulative retention rates for five cohorts of officer and enlisted personnel. Clearly, a single cohort cannot capture the behavioral differences for individual service cohorts.

Figure 3.9 shows the gains that result from inaccuracy in the decrement rate--due mainly to inaccurate continuation rates for military personnel. This is the only category that shows both annual gains and losses that approximately balance between 1986 and 1992. However, sizable gains were realized in FY92-FY94 that can be attributed to the failure to adjust military continuation rates for voluntary separations

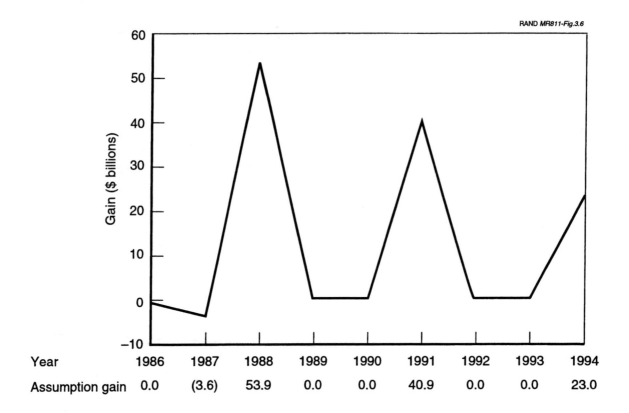

SOURCE: VMRS (1986-1996).

**Figure 3.6--Gains from Changes in Assumptions
and Retirement Structure**

because of the drawdown. Many military personnel with 7-19 years of
service left in FY92-FY94, with voluntary separation payments resulting
in continuation rates that were much lower than those reflected in the
age-entry normal cohort. The voluntary-separation payments to induce
these departures were sizable, but even larger reductions in future
retirement liabilities ensued (Grissmer et al., 1995). A significant
part of these reductions in liabilities was because of service after
October 1, 1984, and therefore part of the registered gains could
arguably be returned to DoD.

A historical example of the problems arising from use of "typical"
cohorts rather than real ones is instructive. Estimates of accrual
payments in 1990-1991 (pre-drawdown) by the actuary show a decreasing

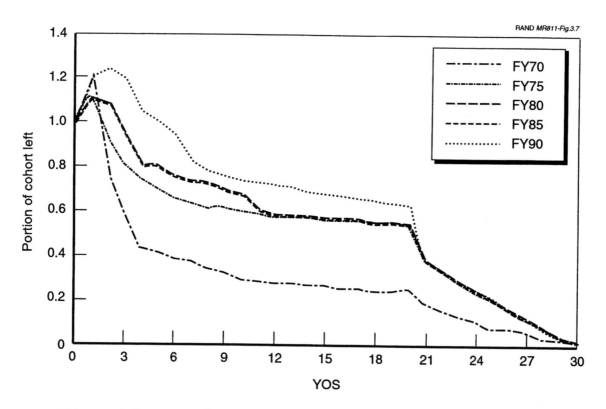

Figure 3.7--Comparison of Cohort Retention Patterns--Officer

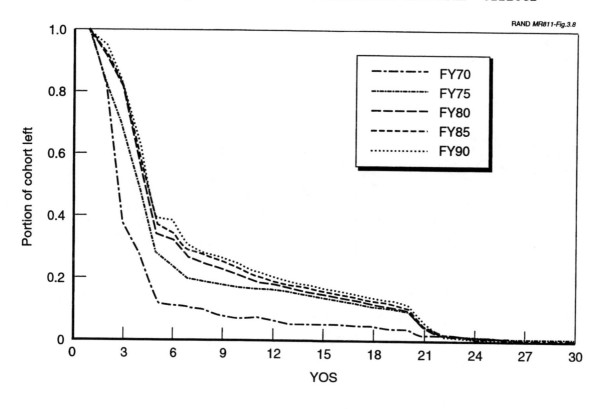

Figure 3.8--Comparison of Cohort Retention Patterns--Enlisted

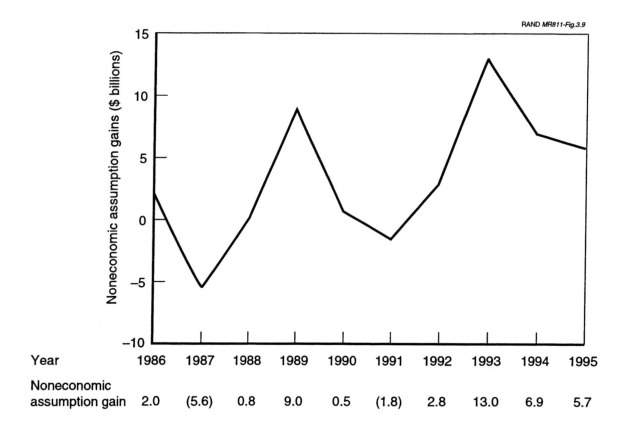

Year	1986	1987	1988	1989	1990	1991	1992	1993	1994	1995
Noneconomic assumption gain	2.0	(5.6)	0.8	9.0	0.5	(1.8)	2.8	13.0	6.9	5.7

SOURCE: VMRS (1986-1996).

Figure 3.9--Gains or (Losses) Due to Non-Economic Assumptions

normal cost from 52 to 44 percent. These figures suggest decreased retirement liabilities. Further investigation would show that the decrease is because of the lower benefits paid to recent and future cohorts. A policymaker might reasonably conclude that retirement liabilities have been reduced through improved management.

Such a conclusion would be wrong. Military retirement liabilities (pre-drawdown) actually would rise because the projected number of retirees would increase significantly. This projected increase in the number of retirees from present and future forces would more than offset the declining retirement benefit and boost retirement liabilities substantially.[7] Such increases are due to the higher retention among cohorts entering since the start of the all-volunteer force and higher

_____

[7]Estimates show that the number of new retirees from active service will double between FY1980 and FY2000.

retention caused by better pay in the 1980s. Thus, the general impression left by a declining NCP is misleading and masks the major source of increasing retirement liabilities: more retirees.

This flaw in the accrual method was present when critical decisions were being made regarding future retention. The method was implemented in 1984 when a number of all-volunteer cohorts were passing through first- and second-term decision points, and the key decisions were made that will lead to the significant increase in the number of new retirees. If stronger incentives had been in place, and DoD accrual payments reflected an increasing number of future retirees, perhaps different decisions would have been made.

Aggregation Bias

The current accrual contributions do not reflect the full retirement cost implications of service or DoD personnel plans. For the services, the accrual contribution from each service reflects not only its personnel plans but also the plans of the other services. This effect occurs because a single NCP is calculated for DoD and applied to each service's budget. Not only does this imply inaccurate estimates for individual services, but it also means that each service cannot derive budget implications without knowing the plans of the others. For DoD, accrual contributions do not reflect full liabilities because the Treasury receives credits and debits from annual gains and losses--even those arising from post-FY84 service.

These inaccuracies will skew decisions made by the services and DoD when attempting to incorporate retirement costs. This means that the Air Force, which has the highest percentage of individuals reaching retirement from a cohort, does not face the full costs of these decisions. The expected result would be increased seniority in the Air Force and a tendency to protect senior airmen from force reductions.

Treasury Bias

The original legislation held DoD accountable for all post-FY84 service but also specified the Treasury as the residual claimant for *all* gains and losses to the system. Congress adopted the latter provision, significantly weakening incentives for DoD to take appropriate personnel actions because it does not fully recoup any savings that result from policies affecting personnel serving after FY84. For instance, holding pay growth below actuarial assumptions would lower retirement liabilities; however, this reduced liability currently would not affect the DoD accrual contribution. More important, restrictions on retention during the planned drawdown would bring large gains to the retirement system, some of which would be reductions in retirement liabilities due to service after October 1, 1984. But this reduction would not reflect in lower DoD accrual contributions.

We should note that the share of changes in unfunded liability that might properly be attributed to DoD will grow as the system ages. All changes in retirement liability will be due to service after October 1, 1984. If DoD does not eventually receive responsibility for changes in liability, DoD managers' incentives to make policy changes would be substantially weakened. One method of allocating these changes to DoD would be to establish a DoD side-amortization account similar to the one in Treasury, to receive such changes in liability. Section Four discusses a second method that recommends a cohort approach incorporating such changes into the annual accrual budget through adjustments in the NCP.

The result of the policy of making Treasury the sole residual claimant has been to make DoD accrual payments significantly larger than they would have been under the alternative policy.

Slow Responsiveness to Change

Another characteristic contributing to the lack of incentives is that both current and prospective retention rates are not incorporated quickly or predictably in accrual calculations. The Board of Actuaries must act to make major changes in entry-age normal continuation rates. If current practice serves as a guide, Board action usually occurs only after large differences have persisted. When such changes are made, no routine method exists for predicting the new assumptions. This is particularly true for changes in retention assumptions. Therefore, the current method responds slowly and unpredictably to changes in retention.

The same is true for adjustments in economic assumptions. Only one significant change was made to economic assumptions in the first eight years of system operation, despite the initial assumptions differing significantly from experience in each of the intervening years. This process creates payment schedules that generally change infrequently but abruptly. The approach effectively eliminates the possibility of immediate feedback through the accrual charge when the retirement liability has changed as a consequence of decisions made by personnel policymakers. Without rapid feedback, the policymakers may be only partly aware of the effects of their decisions on retirement liability and the accrual charge. Such arbitrary procedures do not provide the consistent feedback needed to affect DoD personnel managers.

It may therefore be important to modify the system to reflect projected future policy changes as soon as they can be credibly supported. If a policymaker can expect to see accrual contribution differences in the year in which policies begin, those differences would provide an important impetus for sound policy. This would be possible only if the accrual method incorporates personnel plans and policies prior to implementation. Of course, these plans would need to be credible and consistent with DoD, service, and other budgetary policies.

One reason why prospective incorporation is important is that some personnel policies may actually cost more in the first year. An example is separation pay to achieve drawdown. Separating an individual before retirement generates significant savings in retirement payments. If retirement savings reflect in the year of termination, then they might partially or wholly offset the separation pay and make the policy easier to implement. Thus, DoD would see an immediate benefit in the form of lower accrual contributions when reducing the number of retirees.

Missing Computational Links

Even if the Board of Actuaries increased the system's responsiveness by making annual decisions based on changed assumptions, a personnel planner must still be able to compute the budgetary differences between competing personnel plans to compare them. A personnel planner partially controls retention, promotion, and pay-growth policies. Each of these policy areas will affect retirement liabilities, yet the planner currently has no way to estimate the effect of each of these policies on accrual contributions.

The planner cannot estimate these effects because a clear computational link between future retention rates and entry-age normal retention rates is missing. This gap leaves the rates subject to board intervention, historically an infrequent and unpredictable event. Lacking a clear link, service and OSD policymakers have tended to ignore the consequences.

An example illustrates the current flaws in the system for producing appropriate incentives. Existing policy will reduce the force size substantially over the next five years. Although retirement liabilities will be significantly affected by this drawdown policy, planners do not know how these reduced liabilities will reveal themselves in their accrual budgets. They currently assume that any savings from retirement will only show up in budgets years from now, and thus defense drawdown planning ignores such savings.

If an accrual method that reflected the drawdown immediately and accurately were put into place, several policies might be affected:

- The size of the force reduction required to meet budgetary constraints might be smaller than would occur under the current method.
- Force separations would occur across a more senior group, in place of accession reductions and separation of first-term personnel.
- The level of separation payments given to service members would change and be more efficient (Grissmer et al., 1995) because of offsetting retirement savings in the year of separation.

Fungibility of Accrual Funds

Perhaps the major problem with the accrual method involves the lack of predictable fungibility of accrual funds across other budget categories. Even if all the problems mentioned above were solved, this lack would significantly weaken management incentives.

The problem has its source in the paucity of real funding in the retirement fund. The decision not to provide real funds meant that changes in accrual funding would not affect real outlays and therefore would not be included in any deficit-control legislation. Thus, determining whether changes in the accrual budgets will result in more or less real outlays for DoD requires congressional authority and special consideration every year. If accrual budgets decrease, DoD will still need new real spending authority to convert these savings into spending on other budget items. If accrual budgets increase, DoD does not necessarily lose spending authority in other budget categories. Since accrual budgets have generally declined, the lack of fungibility would mean that such savings would not provide funds for other budget items.

Two documented instances where accrual savings have been translated into real spending authority have occurred (Hix and Taylor, 1997). Both happened when changes in economic assumptions resulted in significant reductions in present and future accrual contributions. In 1986, two changes affecting accrual contributions due to the REDUX system and the estimation of separate NCPs for active and reserve personnel resulted in reductions of over $4 billion. Interestingly, the accrual savings were not returned to the services, in proportion to each service's amount of accrual reduction, but rather were allocated by DoD to top spending priorities. Thus, the precedent was set that accrual reductions go to DoD to be allocated based on spending priorities rather than returned to individual services.

The second instance occurred in 1992 when economic assumptions were reduced, resulting in a reduction of about $15 billion in scheduled accrual contributions over five years. Part of this reduction was legislatively linked to cover voluntary-separation payments made to achieve the drawdown; however, these expenditures were less than $2 billion. DoD, OMB, and Congress negotiated over the remaining accrual savings. The outcome of these negotiations were that the first-year savings were surrendered in exchange for capture of the remaining four-year savings by lifting the top line of the defense budget by the amount of the accrual reduction.[8] Here, the money also reverted to DoD rather than to the services, removing incentives for better management. This solidifies precedent for translation of accrual savings into real spending authority whenever a significant reduction occurs in scheduled contributions, but smaller changes appear to be lost.[9]

The only way that fungibility can be guaranteed to the services is to convert the retirement fund into an advance-funding accrual method. Establishing a trust fund with real dollars would remove any distinction between accrual expenditures and all other expenditures. Such real funding would not only guarantee fungibility, but substantially remove the burden from future generations of paying for past retirement benefits. Such real funding could also make a transition to a defined contribution system where individual service members would own the contributions made on their behalf. The Board of Actuaries has recommended movement to an advance-funding system.

SUMMARY

The current accrual method has probably improved certain aspects of DoD decisionmaking. The major areas where it has contributed are in evaluating and changing the structure of retirement benefits, in making retirement costs more visible, and in providing better retirement costing for active versus reserve personnel. However, it has failed to provide incentives for managing the flow of personnel that determines the proportion of a cohort reaching retirement, for adjusting force size, or for providing incentives to the services by assigning them their own retirement costs. In addition, it has overestimated DoD contributions and failed to return excess payments to DoD as amortized

---

[8]Sean O'Keefe, the DoD comptroller at the time of the negotiation, reports that the top line held for the remaining budget years and he had no doubt that the accrual savings resulted in additional expenditures for those years.

[9]Hix and Taylor (1997) also report an instance where accrual savings of $300 million was explicitly not translated into real budget authority.

gains. Finally, the lack of automatic fungibility in the system creates uncertainty whether gains can be spent and whether the services are treated equitably when gains are returned.

4. STRENGTHENING MANAGEMENT INCENTIVES:
RECOMMENDATIONS FOR CHANGE

We make the following recommendations to address the problems raised in the previous section:

- Improve the quality, timeliness, and accuracy of information available to personnel managers about the consequences of their actions on retirement liabilities by

  - estimating "cohort-specific" NCPs in the entry-age normal methodology

  - using separate NCPs by service for officers and enlisted personnel

  - introducing a more disciplined and informed process of setting future values of economic assumptions and military retention rates by

    -- annually evaluating and updating retention and economic assumptions

    -- incorporating prospective changes in retention and pay when such changes are part of overall defense and national policy and conform to other budget guidance

    -- recognizing historical relationships among the internal economic and retention parameters as reflected by consensus in the research community and relationships between the economic parameters in this method and other macroeconomic parameters used to formulate national budgets.

  - changing the composition of the Board of Actuaries to include representation from economists in the military personnel research community.

- Make managers bear more directly the consequences of their policy changes

  - allocating to DoD rather than Treasury the portion of annual gains and losses in retirement liabilities attributable to service after October 1, 1984

- using separate NCPs by service for officer and enlisted personnel
- returning to the services recovered spending authority from accrual reductions rather than allocating recovered funds at the OSD level
- moving to an advance funded system where fungibility is automatic to each service.

We will describe each of these changes and, where appropriate, estimate their impact on calculations of the normal cost percentage and DoD accrual contributions.

THE COHORT-SPECIFIC ENTRY-AGE NORMAL METHOD

Methodology

The concept of "cohort specific" accrual is straightforward. It simply requires that separate NCPs be estimated for each cohort and used to determine each cohort's accrual contribution. The total DoD annual contribution is then simply the sum of all cohort contributions. This technique is conceptually equivalent to establishing an independent retirement fund for each cohort. The method will provide actuarially sound funding for each cohort, and thus will provide actuarially sound funding for the whole system.

The formula below illustrates the methodology. For a *beginning* cohort, an NCP can be estimated based on the same entry age normal techniques currently used. Future assumptions for the cohort can be made similar to the method currently used. This NCP can be used to calculate the accrual contribution from this cohort to this year's total DoD contribution. This contribution is simply equal to the total cohort pay in its first year times the NCP. The formula is:

$$NCP(j) = PVFB(j)/PVFP \qquad (2)$$

where

Present Value of Future Benefits (PVFB) is $\quad \Sigma_i \, R_i \, B_{ij} \, D_i$

and

Present Value of Future Pay (PVFP) is $\quad \Sigma_i \, A_i \, P_i \, D_i$

where

i = years since entry

j = retirement benefit category

R_i = number of retirees in year i

B_{ij} = average retirement benefit in year i for benefit
category j

D_i = discount factor from year i to entry

A_i = number on active duty in year i

P_i = average pay in year i

Fiscal Year NCP = $\sum_j W_j \, NCP(j)$

where

W_j = proportion of total base pay received in current
fiscal year by benefit category j.

For previous-year cohorts, the NCP required for sound funding can
be calculated using actual retention and economic data, with future
values again set by assumptions. This use of historical data implicitly
assumes that future contributions from a cohort are determined as if a
fund had existed over the life of the cohort. The previous
contributions from this cohort are assumed to be determined by the
current NCP applied against the appropriate historical total base pay
for each year of the cohort's life. These contributions are assumed to
have earned interest at historical interest rates.

This presumed existence of a past fund is a way to determine the
level of future contributions from each cohort in the force in FY84.
The levels of these contributions are important, for they determine how
cohort retirement liabilities should divide between the DoD and
Treasury. This division can be determined for each cohort by assuming
that contributions occurring after FY84 contribute to the DoD liability,
and those during or prior to FY84 reduce the unfunded Treasury
liability.

At the initiation of the accrual method in 1984, the initial NCPs
to charge to each cohort could have been calculated using the procedures
described above. The initial annual DoD contribution could have been

calculated by applying the cohort-specific NCPs to the FY85 total pay in each cell (see formula 2 above) and then summing vertically across cohorts.

If all assumptions made in the initial calculation were accurate, then the same NCPs would be used each year but applied against the succeeding year's force to arrive at annual DoD contributions. But the assumptions are rarely very accurate, and the process needs a procedure to correct for inaccuracies. The required NCP for each cohort will change each year if new actual data does not match assumptions, if future assumptions are changed from the preceding year's, or if the structure of benefits changes.

If changes occur for any of these reasons, then past contributions were either over- or underfunded. The method needs a procedure to divide this gain or loss between Treasury and DoD and to reflect the DoD portion in future DoD payments. The division between Treasury and DoD can be done by computing a new NCP that incorporates the updated data and other changes in assumptions or benefits. The new NCP represents what should have been charged over the life of the cohort. The two sums can be compared to determine the extent of correction required. Each cohort's past streams can be identified by whether the contribution occurred for service before or after October 1, 1984, and the difference proportionally allocated between DoD and the Treasury.[1]

Two methods can reflect DoD's identified portion in future DoD contributions. The first incorporates the adjustment entirely in future NCPs, while the second establishes a side amortization account to receive all or part of the gain or loss. In the first method, a third NCP is calculated, which is the level percentage required over the *remaining life* of the cohort to maintain sound funding of the DoD liability. Using this method, the NCPs are adjusted each year based on actual numbers and incorporate changed assumptions and benefits. These

---

[1]An important issue in assigning gains and losses to DoD is whether DoD has control over their source. Gains and losses arising from retention rates therefore are clearly under DoD control, while interest rates are not. One can argue that gains and losses arising from factors outside DoD control be assigned to Treasury. These issues are discussed further in Hix and Taylor, 1997.

adjustments are just sufficient to keep each cohort with actuarially sound funding scheduled over the remainder of the cohort's life.

Because approximately 30 cohorts are present in any year, the average period for "amortizing" the gain or loss is approximately 15 years. However, adjustments are likely to be larger for more recent cohorts, so the effective amortization period is probably longer. This adjustment period partially protects the accrual contribution from undue volatility.

The second method for adjusting the payment stream is to establish a DoD side-amortization account--similar to the current Treasury account--that receives the DoD portion of gains or losses. In this case, the amortization period can be set by assumption, and the new NCP is calculated as in the first method but eliminates that portion of the gain or loss being amortized.

Advantages of the Cohort Approach

The standard entry-age normal method differs from the cohort method by substituting a "typical" cohort for each of the actual historical and future cohorts. If the data vary little over the years, the two techniques will produce similar accrual contributions. However, if retention, COLAs, pay growth, and interest rates vary significantly, then the typical cohort method is likely to generate substantial annual gains and losses.

In situations with greater levels of variance, cohort accounting has an advantage in terms of providing incentives. It does not assume steady-state behavior, because each cohort calculation includes the cohort's actual data. This method's calculations are more accurate because

- It uses actual historical rather than "typical" cohort data.
- It can project future retention for specific cohorts.
- It allows easy division of gains and losses into Treasury and DoD portions.
- It requires annual updating of data and assumptions and therefore identifies and incorporates trends more quickly.

The option to incorporate cohort-specific retention projections has a decided advantage for producing more-accurate accrual estimates. Research has established that cohort retention rates can differ substantially depending on the demographic composition of the cohort, its size, the retirement benefits available, and its particular retention and promotion history. Using such information could reduce the gains and losses encountered each year.

Creating incentives to incorporate retirement costs is more important in manpower systems that exhibit large variance in key parameters. These changes can imply rapid changes in manpower costs that require policy intervention to keep those costs at appropriate levels.

The cohort method has strong advantages here also. It produces improved incentives because accrual contributions respond annually to changed behavior and assumptions, and prospective changes in policy can be incorporated in detail into each cohort's computation. In addition, planners can be provided with easily run algorithms that can produce accurate estimates of the effect of different personnel plans on accrual contributions. Thus, budget planners probably will include the accrual calculations because they will change year to year in response to policy; this is possible because the methods use straightforward computations.

DEVELOP SEPARATE NORMAL COST PERCENTAGES BY SERVICE FOR OFFICER AND ENLISTED PERSONNEL

Service-specific accrual contributions do not reflect service-specific retention rates or retirement liabilities. This is a major source of system inaccuracy. If the services had similar NCPs and similar officer/enlisted ratios, then the additional work required to develop separate NCPs would not be worthwhile. However, large differences in service-specific liabilities result both from differing probabilities of enlisted and officer cohorts reaching retirement and different mixes of officer and enlisted personnel. For instance, Figure 3.1 shows the projected percentages of entering enlisted cohorts reaching retirement. Somewhat smaller--but still significant--differences exist for officers across services.

A second problem is that officers have much higher cohort retirement probabilities than do enlisted personnel. Different officer/enlisted mixes by service therefore will result in inaccurate estimates by service. Because of higher retention rates and a higher officer/enlisted mix, the Air Force retires proportionately almost twice as many as the other services, yet the services' accrual contributions do not reflect this difference.

SETTING MORE-ACCURATE ASSUMPTIONS

The computation of NCPs depends, in part, on two general categories of assumptions: one pertaining to retention and the other to economic assumptions. The second category includes assumptions about pay growth, COLAs, and interest rates. NCPs (and therefore accrual contributions) are extremely sensitive to both categories of assumptions. Figure 4.1 shows the effect of lowering the pay-growth assumption from 5.75 to 4.75 percent. The result is slightly less than a billion-dollar difference in the DoD annual accrual contribution in the first few years, but over

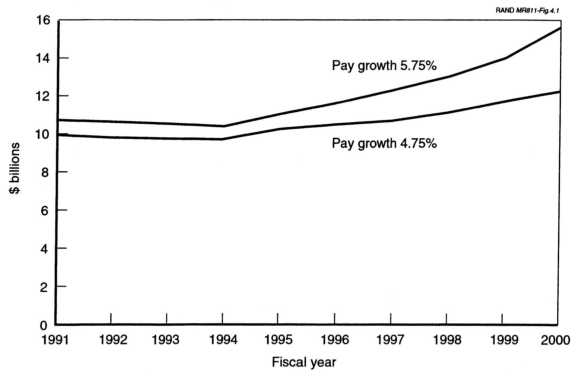

Figure 4.1--Effect of Changing Economic Assumptions on DoD Contributions

$3 billion annually in the longer term. Interest and COLA assumptions also show strong effects, albeit less than that of pay growth.

If these parameters had been historically constant, then the sensitivity would not be an important issue. However, each of the economic assumptions, as well as retention rates, displays substantial variance over the past 20 years, and it is not unreasonable to assume they will continue to do so.

Assumptions involve two distinct time periods--near and long term. For some parameters, long term projections extend for 40-50 years. The distinction between the periods is important for two reasons. First, near-term values are easier to predict than long-term values, and different methods should be used to generate them. Second, accrual contributions are more sensitive to changes in a near-term annual value in a given year. For instance, a 5-percent pay raise tomorrow affects contributions more than does a similar raise five years from now.

The history of assumptions has shown significant differences between actual values and assumptions, as Figures 3.2-3.4 illustrated. For an actuarial system designed only to ensure payments, the emphasis is not on whether individual parameters are in error so much as whether the net effect of the assumptions produces significant misfunding. Errors in individual assumptions may not be serious because they can be changed gradually to restore sound funding. In these types of systems, assumptions are seen as the control mechanisms to guide the fund to avoid substantial misfunding. But in an accrual system where annual accuracy is necessary to reflect true costs and provide incentives, accurate projections of each parameter are important. The following actions will increase projection accuracy:

- Incorporate the prospective effects of policy actions on parameter values.
- Modify the retention-rate projections to incorporate the retention history and composition of each cohort, relationships between projected economic parameters and retention, and the effects of changes in end-strength and other policies.

• Use more-sophisticated relationships and techniques developed in the economic and statistical literature to project economic parameters.

Incorporating the Effect of Policy Actions

The incorporation of potential effects of policy actions must be handled prudently, with the understanding that prospective actions are not always carried out and that "gaming" of the system can occur. If prospective policies were automatically included in near-term retention estimates, then planners could institute policies for the explicit purpose of reducing near-term contributions at the expense of raising long-term contributions. Judgments therefore must be made by an independent and impartial group regarding whether prospective policies are likely enough to be implemented that including calculations regarding them would improve the accuracy of near-term estimates.

Those making these judgments should consider whether the policies are part of a broader policy framework extending beyond specific services, as well as the track record of individual services in carrying out previous policies. Drawdown, for instance, is a clear congressional and administration policy addressing the apparent collapse of the Warsaw Pact threat. While the specific details and retention effects of the policy may not be predictable with great accuracy, recognizing some part of the drawdown would provide more-accurate projections than would ignoring it. These judgements are better made by labor economists with expertise in military-personnel labor markets than by actuarial scientists.

As part of the budget process, prospective policies are often provided in detail over the following six years. For instance, end strengths, pay levels, and personnel force structures are routine parts of budget submissions. Automatic incorporation of these policy effects into accrual assumptions may not be warranted. However, ignoring these effects will probably lead to more inaccuracy than their incorporation would.

Improving Retention Estimates

Retention estimates can also be improved considerably by incorporation of demographic composition, previous retention history, and potential effects of changes in pay levels and general economic conditions. These effects have been thoroughly researched, and more-accurate projections can result from incorporation of the results. Again, the expertise to make these judgments lies in the economic (rather than actuarial) community.

Improved Economic Models

Near-term projections of economic parameters might be improved through incorporation of information and predictions arising from macro-economic models, or estimation through time-series analysis of separate relationships between these parameters and other, more easily predicted parameters. The longer-term projections of these parameters might also be improved, although accurate longer-term projections from econometric models are more problematic.

Finally, the models and assumptions used to produce future projections should be internally consistent. For instance, falling or rising interest rates usually occur in conjunction with particular phases of the economic cycle. Economic cycles markedly affect retention and likely would affect pay raises and COLAs. Projections of each of these parameters should show an internal consistency that flows from a common future economic scenario.

CHANGING THE COMPOSITION OF THE BOARD OF ACTUARIES

Implementing many of the actions described above will require judgments in the following areas:

- the appropriateness of choice of various models and model specifications for projecting parameters in the short and long term
- the extent to which various prospective personnel policies should be included in projections
- the internal consistency of the various projections.

Individuals with backgrounds in manpower planning or labor economics will construct more-accurate projections. The governing body for the accrual method should include members from wider disciplinary backgrounds with its actuaries. Actuarially sound funding methods are still required for the system, but improvement in accuracy of estimates and management incentives requires the participation of those possessing the above skills.

The reconstituted governing board should maintain an independence from the DoD, as the present board has. This independence is preserved by long terms of service, appointment by the President, and accountability to Congress.

DoD PARTICIPATION IN GAINS AND LOSSES

As we pointed out in Section 3, the original legislation allows two interpretations concerning the disposition of annual gains and losses to the system. The interpretation selected accrued all gains and losses to the Treasury. No provision was made for a side-amortization account or other procedure to assign gains or losses to DoD. In the long term, the absence of a DoD side account or equivalent procedure is inconsistent with the goal of having DoD assume full responsibility for all retirement liabilities after 60 years. Such an account would have to be created.

Creating it now makes sense, because it strengthens incentives for improved management. Without such an account or procedure, policy changes that are not prospectively anticipated in accrual calculations will not affect DoD contributions. It means, for instance, that the total change in liabilities for an unanticipated drawdown or force buildup would fall to Treasury. Such a procedure actually produces perverse incentives within DoD to produce losses that get assigned to Treasury.

For these reasons, we believe the method of amortizing gains and losses to the system in the absence of moving to a cohort method should be changed to include a DoD amortization account or equivalent procedure that reflects changes due to service after October 1, 1984. The cohort-specific entry-age normal method provides a way to incorporate gains and losses into future NCPs, and a side account would be unnecessary. If a side account is set up, the amortization period for this account should probably be set much lower than the Treasury amortization account, to provide more-rapid feedback and strengthened incentives for efficient management of manpower.[2]

SEPARATE NORMAL COST PERCENTAGES BY SERVICE AND OFFICER/ENLISTED

Service-specific NCPs for officer and enlisted personnel offer the best solution because they make service decisionmakers responsible for their own--and only their own--retirement liabilities. Currently, decisionmakers in each service do not bear the consequences of their actions partly because their accrual contributions do not reflect differences in cohort-retirement probabilities or officer/enlisted mixes. Because the Air Force has a higher officer/enlisted mix and higher cohort-retirement probabilities, its retirement costs are currently subsidized by other services, mainly the Army (Hix and Taylor, 1997). These subsidies reduce the incentives for the Air Force to restrain seniority.

ENSURING FUNGIBILITY AT THE SERVICE LEVEL

The history involving the recapture of accrual savings for real spending authority shows that major gains have been recaptured, while smaller gains have not. However, the services experience considerable uncertainty whether future gains will be recaptured, because such depends on the fiscal environment and negotiations between DoD, OMB, and Congress. Moreover, historical precedent indicates that previous major gains were considered to revert to OSD rather than to the services.

---

[2]The Board of Actuaries has recommended the establishment of a DoD side account for distributing gains for service after 1984. However, Congress has not acted on the request (DoD, Retirement Board of Actuaries, 1992). The length of the amortization period is critical to establishing management incentives. The current 30-year period used for amortization of Treasury payments would provide virtually no incentive if used for DoD gains. The Board has suggested both a method of recapturing DoD gains for service after 1984 and a method for amortizing those gains. Alternative methods have also been suggested (Hix and Taylor, 1997).

Such gains have been used to fund priority items determined by the OSD rather than revert to the services in proportion to their accrual gains.

The only way to make accrual gains and losses fungible at the service level is to create an advance-funding system. This would increase the deficit (or decrease the budget surplus) in the short run, but would have several benefits in the longer term. First, it would probably cover part of its costs through more-efficient personnel management. Second, it would remove the intergenerational transfers implicit in the current method. These transfers can place future retirement payments at more risk because of their dependence on future generations to pay the obligations. Burdened with social security obligations, future generations may opt to reduce benefits through lower COLAs rather than pay the full implicit benefit. Advance funding when budget surpluses are possible would protect future benefits from such risks.

Third, the federal employees' retirement systems, and most private-sector retirement systems, are becoming defined contribution systems with real contributions in accounts controlled by employees. Presumably, this movement is fueled by concerns for efficiency and the risk of large, uncertain future obligations. This will make the military retirement system increasingly visible, probably increasing the future political risk associated with retirement benefits. Advance funding would ease the transition to such defined contribution systems.

Fourth, military-compensation research suggests that a more cost-effective mix of personnel could be produced by higher retention of those with 4-12 years of service and reduced retention of those with 12-20 (Asch and Warner, 1994a). Alternative military retirement systems have been proposed to achieve this (Asch and Warner, 1994b). These recommendations would also move toward the characteristics of defined contribution systems with individual ownership of funds, with earlier implicit partial vesting occurring during years 4-12. While it is possible for such systems to operate within the parameters of the current method, an advance-funding method would provide more flexibility for individual control of funds, such as that offered by the Federal Employees Retirement System.

5. FISCAL IMPACT OF RAND RECOMMENDATIONS

In this section, we estimate future contributions to the military retirement fund for enlisted personnel in the near term using the cohort method, and compare these with using the actuary's methods[1] in FY90. We explain the large difference in estimates. Finally, we present more-recent estimates using current actuarial methods based on a new set of economic assumptions adopted in July 1992 and FY94.

ASSUMPTIONS

Two RAND estimates using different assumptions were made of accrual contributions in FY91-FY99. The first assumes no drawdown and the second assumes a significant drawdown of active forces. The drawdown is incorporated in the RAND cohort method by incorporating changing continuation rates by cohort that take into account both the reduced end strength and the method of reaching that end strength. For these calculations, we have assumed that the drawdown is accomplished by a combination of accession reductions and increased attrition from the enlisted force. The increased attrition is assumed to occur primarily through voluntary-separation incentives offered to enlisted personnel.[2] We assume that accession levels are not allowed to fall below 90 percent of the long-term, steady-state level required to sustain the reduced force size[3] (Grissmer et al., 1995).

---

[1]The FY90 actuarial estimates are simulations made by RAND using the actuarial methodology--but not including survivor benefits in either estimate. Thus, the actuarial estimates presented here will not exactly match published estimates.

[2]Congress authorized voluntary-separation incentives in FY92 for individuals with 7-20 years of service. The individuals offered incentives were given a choice between a lump-sum payment and an annuity. The lump sum is equal to 15 percent of base pay for each year of service; the annuity is paid for a number of years equal to twice the years of service and is equal to .025 × years of service × base pay. The annuity is not adjusted for cost of living.

[3]The OSD guidelines to the services with respect to the drawdown specified that accession levels were not to fall below 90 percent of steady-state levels.

Both RAND estimates also make the following assumptions:

- Future economic and mortality assumptions match those of the Board of Actuaries.
- Future post-drawdown continuation rates are the average of FY87-FY89.
- The three retirement plans of FP, HI-3, and REDUX are incorporated by cohort.

The assumptions of the Board of Actuaries appear in its annual report for FY90.[4] It assumes a single set of continuation rates for all cohorts. The economic assumptions used by both methods for the FY90 estimates are COLAs of 5 percent, military pay growth of 6.25 percent, and interest of 6.6 percent. The board changed economic assumptions in its meeting in July 1992. The changes in assumptions raised interest to 7.0 percent and lowered military pay growth to 5.5 percent.

RESULTS WITH FY90 ECONOMIC ASSUMPTIONS

Figure 5.1 contrasts the RAND estimates of the NCP with no drawdown with the actuarial estimates. The estimates not only show significantly lower estimates using the RAND method, but also show differing trends in future contributions. The actuarial estimates show a declining NCP, while the RAND estimates show an increasing NCP.

The actuarial estimates decline primarily because of the reduction in retirement benefits under HI-1 and REDUX, which a greater proportion of retirees will be receiving in future years. Figure 5.2 shows the NCP calculated by the actuary for the three different benefit cohorts. The data show significant reductions in the NCP required to support the HI-1 and REDUX plans. The actuary weighs the three NCPs using the current proportion of base pay paid to individuals in the three groups to arrive at the overall NCP. The reduction in value of the military retirement benefit from FP to REDUX means that the NCP will decline as a greater proportion of individuals in service qualify under the new formulas. In FY90, those with more than 10 years of service would qualify under FP,

---

[4]DoD, Office of the Actuary, *VMRS*, 1988.

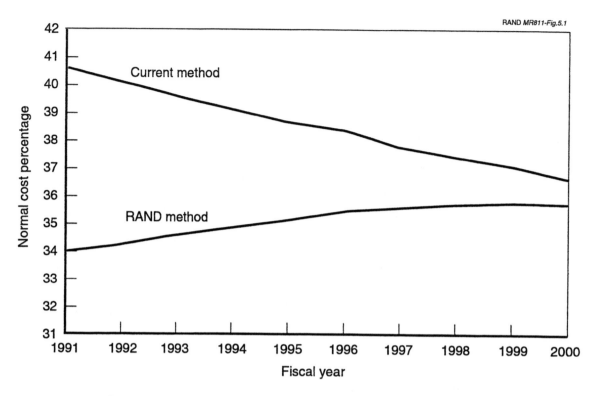

Figure 5.1--Comparison of the RAND and Actuary NCP

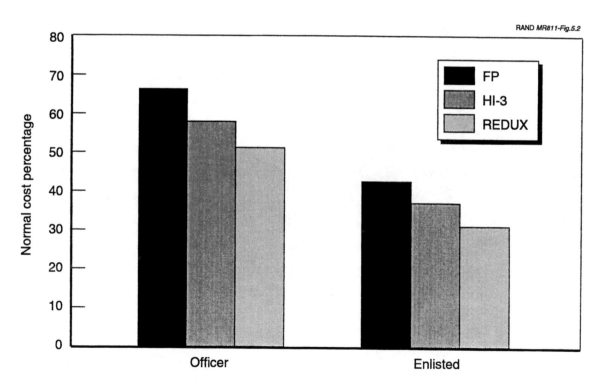

Figure 5.2--Comparison of NCP for the Three Retirement Structures

while those with between 4 and 10 would be HI-1 and those with less than 4 years of service would qualify for REDUX. Because the younger years-of-service groups are significantly larger than older groups, most of the effect of the reduced benefit will occur in the 1990s.

The RAND method incorporates the effect of reduced retirement benefits. However, the RAND method also incorporates the effect of increasing continuation rates during 1970-1990, which will substantially increase the number of retiring military personnel. Figure 2.9 shows estimates of the proportion of entering cohorts retiring for 1970-1990. The estimates use actual data through 1990 for each cohort and assume future continuation rates to be the average of FY87-FY89. One reason for the increasing NCP in the RAND method is that it accounts for the increasing proportion of retiring cohorts. The actuarial estimates use a single set of continuation rates for estimating an NCP and thus cannot take into account the dynamic changes in cohort retention.

Besides incorporating higher cohort retention, the RAND method accounts for historical economic data. Figure 5.3 shows the military pay-growth assumptions used by RAND and the actuary. RAND uses the actual pay growth experienced by cohorts up to FY90 and then assumes the current actuarial assumption of 5.8 percent for future years. The actuary effectively assumes a 5.8-percent pay growth for all cohorts. The data show that historical pay growth for the cohorts currently in the force is significantly below 5.8 percent, and the effect of this in the cohort method is to reduce the NCP needed to fund the retirement system. Figure 5.4 shows similar comparisons for interest rates. Historical interest rates have been higher than actuarial assumptions, and this also will result in lower NCPs in the cohort method.

Figure 5.5 shows the effect of estimating separate NCPs for each service. The primary beneficiaries of separating service contributions will be the Marine Corps, Army, and Navy. FY91 NCPs for these services would drop from 41 percent to 28-31 percent. Even the Air Force would have a lower NCP in FY91-FY93 because of the overall lowered contributions (but would pay more in FY94-FY99). The service differences in NCP are primarily due to the different proportions of entering cohorts reaching retirement in the four services. In

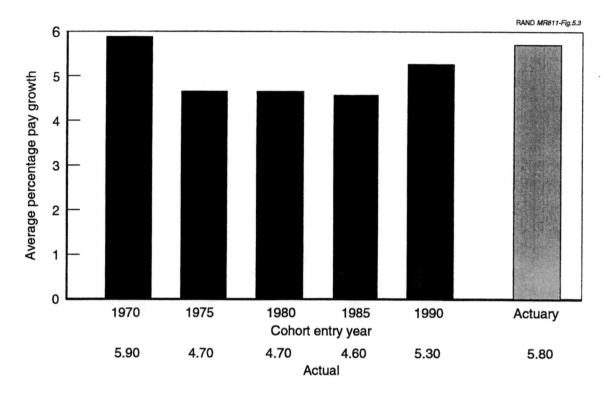

Figure 5.3--Comparison of Actual Pay Growth and
Actuarial Assumption for Cohorts

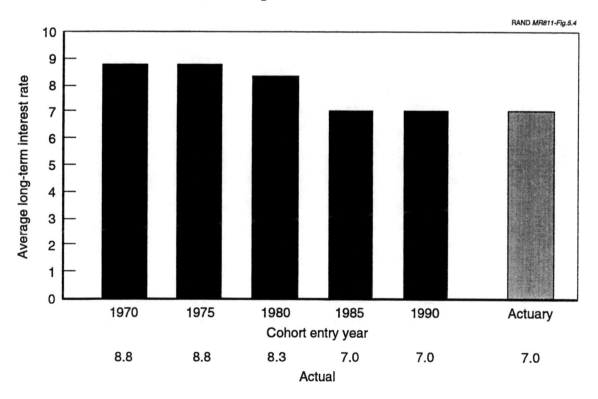

Figure 5.4--Comparison of Actual Interest Rates and Actuarial
Rates for Cohorts

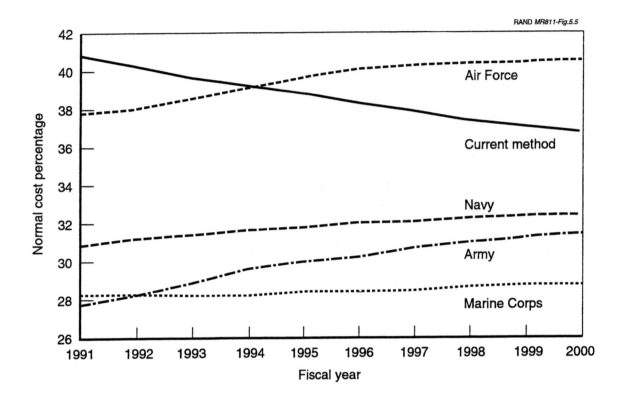

RAND MR811-Fig.5.5

Figure 5.5--Comparison of RAND Estimates by Service with Actuarial Estimates

FY91-FY97, the Army contribution would average $32 billion annually with the current method, but only $24 billion under the RAND method.

Figure 5.6 contrasts the RAND estimates, including the drawdown, with the previous estimates. The drawdown lowers the NCP by about 2 percentage points from the RAND estimate without the drawdown. The lower NCP is the result of a smaller number of retirements occurring among individuals currently in the force with between 7 and 19 years of service. We assume these individuals take voluntary-separation offers to leave and forgo retirement.

Figure 5.7 shows the current dollar amount of accrual reductions due to the drawdown. Accrual savings of nearly $1 billion per year would result from the assumed drawdown. However, the separation-pay costs to achieve these voluntary separations partially offset these savings. Unfortunately, the current accrual system cannot incorporate drawdown effects directly into its methodology, and the effects of the drawdown will only be felt in the long term as actual continuation rates

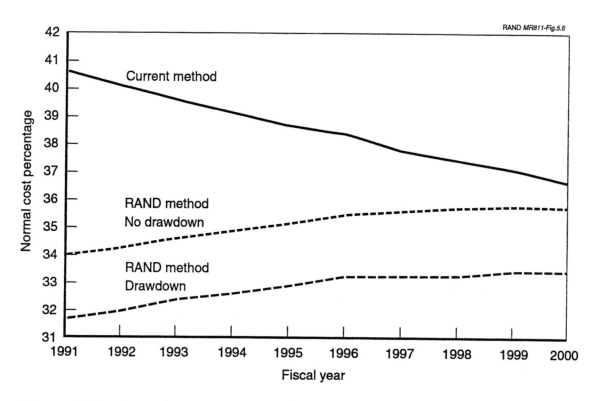

Figure 5.6--Comparison of RAND Estimates With and Without the Drawdown

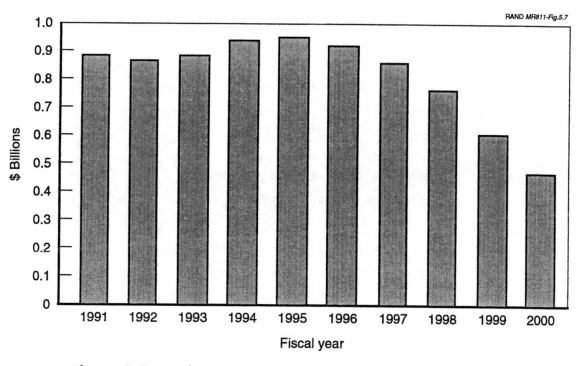

Figure 5.7--Estimated Accrual Savings from the Drawdown

during the drawdown become incorporated into the synthetic cohort. This will not occur for 10 or more years.

The cohort method can incorporate drawdown effects simultaneously with the drawdown and could allow separation payments to be offset by accrual reductions. This would provide motivation for the services to separate voluntarily more-senior personnel without incurring additional costs. If the services do not draw down the force across all experience levels, future forces will likely encounter shortages of senior personnel because of the small number of cohorts enlisted during the drawdown. Thus, the failure of the accrual method to reflect changing retirement liabilities accurately and quickly can affect the experience mix of the force today and in the future.

Figure 5.8 contrasts RAND estimates of accrual contributions incorporating the drawdown with FY90 actuarial estimates. The savings using the cohort method and incorporating the drawdown are about $4 billion in FY92, declining to $2.5 billion in FY97. Over the six-year period shown, the reduction in accrual payments is approximately $17 billion.

We emphasize that the cohort methodology would not necessarily provide lower estimates than the current method in future years. If force increases or other situations arise that would increase continuation rates, DoD payments would increase more quickly than they would under the current method.

Results with New FY92 and FY94 Economic Assumptions

The Board of Actuaries changed the economic assumptions in FY92 and again in FY94. The established board policy for changing economic assumptions was every five years. The first change in assumptions occurred in FY89, five years after the initiation of the system. The next scheduled change was to be in FY94. However, the board chose to change assumptions sooner, perhaps to recognize the effects of the drawdown, or to recognize previous levels of overfunding or excessively conservative assumptions.[5] Figure 5.9 shows the new and old actuarial

---

[5]RAND estimates of accrual contributions were substituted for the board estimates for FY94-FY97 in the FY92 budget submissions by OMB.

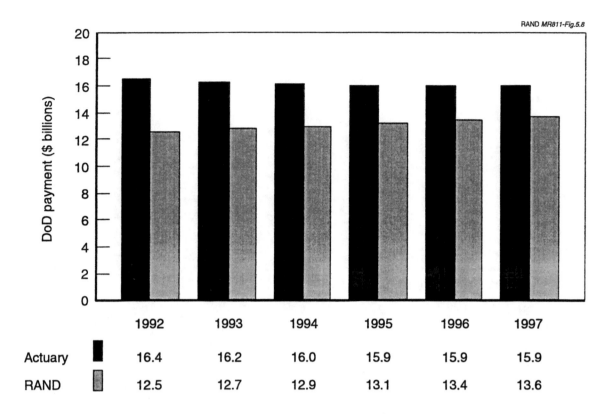

RAND *MR811-Fig.5.8*

	1992	1993	1994	1995	1996	1997
Actuary	16.4	16.2	16.0	15.9	15.9	15.9
RAND	12.5	12.7	12.9	13.1	13.4	13.6

Figure 5.8--Comparison of RAND Accrual Payments to the Actuary

contributions, together with the FY90 RAND estimates. The changed assumptions bring the new actuarial estimates closer to the RAND estimates made in FY90. However, if the new economic assumptions reflect better estimates of future conditions, then RAND estimates incorporating these new assumptions will also show significant reductions. Thus, a gap will still exist between the new actuarial

---

These estimates would have required reconciliation by Congress in the FY94 authorization process. The assumption changed by the board came close to reconciling the two estimates.

Another factor influencing the board assumptions was comparisons with assumptions in private-sector systems. Private pension funds are monitored by the IRS for excessive levels of contributions and possible sheltering of profits from taxation. Funds are monitored using the concept of a "spread" that is defined as the difference in interest and pay-growth assumption. Spreads lower than 1.25 indicate the possibility of excess contributions. Spreads of 1.5-2.0 are generally considered to be sufficiently conservative to maintain actuarial soundness. The board assumptions up to July 1992 had spreads of 1 or less, a level that if maintained in the private sector would have triggered IRS review. The new assumptions have a spread of 1.5 percent.

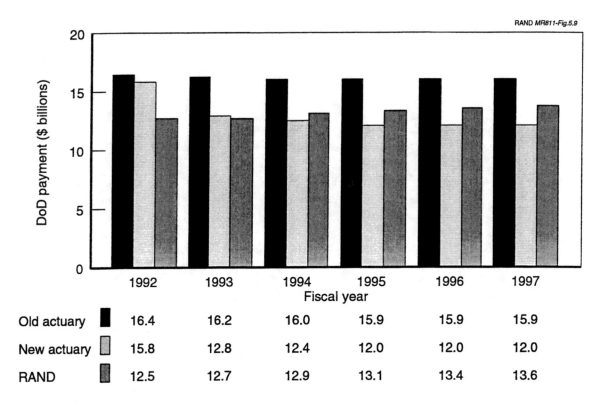

RAND *MR811-Fig.5.9*

	1992	1993	1994	1995	1996	1997
Old actuary	16.4	16.2	16.0	15.9	15.9	15.9
New actuary	15.8	12.8	12.4	12.0	12.0	12.0
RAND	12.5	12.7	12.9	13.1	13.4	13.6

Figure 5.9--Comparison of RAND Estimates (FY90 Assumptions) with Board Estimates with New 1992 and 1994 Assumptions

estimates and the RAND estimates using the cohort method with the drawdown and new economic assumptions. The gap will still be present because the board still does not explicitly incorporate the drawdown or the effect of different historical retention and economic parameters.

Impact on Policy and Discretionary Spending

The DoD, in agreement with the OMB,[6] replaced the Board of Actuary estimates with the RAND estimates of accrual contributions in the President's budget submitted to Congress in FY92. The difference over the five-year planning horizon was approximately $15 billion. The President's budget assumed that this difference was discretionary money and allowed the defense budget for procurement, readiness, and other personnel expenditures to be $15 billion higher.

---

[6]RAND presented several briefings of our results; audiences included the Board of Actuaries and the DoD Actuary, the Assistant Secretary of Defense (Force Management and Policy), the Director (Program Analysis and Evaluation), and OMB personnel.

An outside panel consisting of two actuaries and two economists[7] was appointed to examine RAND's estimates and its recommendations for changing the accrual system. The motivation for making the changes in the President's budget was partly to provide a temporary solution to the problem of a declining defense budget. However, the replacement was also made because RAND estimates were perceived as a more accurate reflection of DoD retirement liabilities in an era of drawdown. The replacement also highlighted what was perceived as a history of excessive DoD contributions to the retirement fund because of conservative assumptions and the lack of a mechanism to return excessive contributions to DoD.

The report of the panel[8] recommended changing the conservative assumptions used to date. It concluded that use of the board's current economic assumptions in the private sector would trigger Internal Revenue Service review for excessive contributions to retirement plans to escape taxation. This recommendation led to the changes in economic assumptions made in July 1992. The panel also recommended establishing a mechanism to return part of the annual gains to DoD, although this would take congressional approval. It did not recommend moving to a cohort methodology, mainly because the actuarial profession does not have a professionally accepted cohort approach to accrual accounting.[9] Finally, it did not recommend moving to a service-specific approach because of the additional computational burdens.[10]

---

[7]The members were John Grady, Principal Actuary, Coopers and Lybrand, and member of the DoD Board of Actuaries; Sam Gutterman, Senior Manager, Price Waterhouse; Kathleen Utgoff, former head of Employee Retirement Income Security Act (ERISA); and Carolyn Weaver, Resident Scholar, American Enterprise Institute.

[8]John H. Grady, Sam Gutterman, Kathleen P. Utgoff, and Carolyn Weaver, "Panel Report on RAND Recommendations for Changes in the Calculation of Accrual Payments to Fund Military Retirement," Washington, D.C.: April 23, 1992.

[9]None of the professionally accepted methods used by actuaries to fund retirement systems uses a cohort approach. This can be a serious methodological failure in a time of industry downsizing and more-rapid and dynamic turnover of the labor force within industries.

[10]Our recommendations called for incorporating separate continuation rates by service in estimating service accrual payments. The actuaries envisioned having to change every decrement rate by service (mortality, survivor benefits, etc.). From an incentive

The issue of the fungibility of this $15-billion reduction was explicitly addressed in negotiations among OSD, OMB, and Congress. First, the obligations incurred as a result of one type of separation payment--the Variable Separation Incentive (VSI)--were offset by accrual reductions through specific legislative authority. VSI was an annuity offered to service members to leave service voluntarily. DoD was ordered to pay for the annuity through an accrual mechanism that could specifically be funded through reductions in the retirement accrual account. Thus, DoD needed no new budget authority to pay for VSIs whose costs would amount to $1-$2 billion.[11]

Second, negotiations between OMB, DoD, and Congress resulted in increasing the top line of the defense budget in the four outyears by exactly the amount of the accrual reductions providing DoD additional spending authority in those years.[12] Third, the spending authority associated with the accrual account (almost all is spent in the same fiscal year) meant that DoD could fund a different and preferred mix of procurement and readiness accounts, easing a fiscal crisis related to deficit-reduction concerns. Because procurement items were highest on the priority list, the availability of the additional spending authority probably meant recovery of more spending authority than indicated by the four outyears.

---

viewpoint, it is only necessary to incorporate those parameters under service control: continuation rates.

[11]Unfortunately, VSI was one of two separation incentives to be offered to service personnel. The other incentive--SSI--was paid in a lump sum and was preferred by enlisted personnel and much less so by officers. SSI payments were not explicitly offset by declining accrual payments. However, VSI offsets were $1-$2 billion.

[12]Sean O'Keefe, the retiring DoD comptroller at the time, reported this result in conversations, stating that those top-line numbers held in future years--thereby implicitly providing more spending authority.

6. CONCLUSIONS

The current accrual method has been partially effective in helping DoD better manage one component of retirement liabilities--the structure and level of the military retirement benefit. The reduction in military retirement benefits that took place in 1986 probably would not have occurred if an accrual method had not been in place. Moreover, the accrual method has provided more readily available estimates of retirement costs that can be used when making certain long-term tradeoff decisions involving substitution of civilian and military personnel, or substitution of capital for labor. To the extent that these kinds of decisions are made and incorporate accurate accrual estimates of retirement costs, it is likely that those decisions are better made. But the accrual estimates of retirement costs to date have significantly overestimated these costs; therefore, their inclusion also significantly biases these substitutions.

Furthermore, the current accrual method is ineffective in influencing the other major components of retirement liabilities--the number of individuals reaching retirement eligibility. Our analysis concludes that, partly due to contradictions in the legislation and partly due to implementation decisions the Board of Actuaries made, the management incentives needed to effect year-to-year personnel decisions that influence the future number of retirees are largely absent from the current method. The method does not link changes in DoD retirement liabilities to changes in the accrual payments made by DoD or the services. Therefore, service personnel managers treat the accrual payments as exogenous--that is, not under their control--and thus retirement costs are essentially excluded from management consideration on a year-to-year basis.

Although the accrual method establishes different retirement costs for active and reserve personnel, a major flaw in the system is that retirement costs are not estimated specifically for each military service. This practice results in significantly higher payments by the Army and significantly lower payments by the Air Force, a net subsidy of the Air Force by the Army. From FY91 through FY97, service-specific payments by the Army, as estimated in FY91, would be $32 billion using the actuary's method, but only $24 billion using the RAND method. Changing this aspect of the method does not require congressional legislation, but can be effected by a Board of Actuaries decision.

Moreover, the current method has set DoD payments too high, and does not return overpayments to DoD through lowered future payments. Instead, all actuarial gains are assigned to Treasury payments. This flaw would have little effect if the annual estimates of liabilities were random--sometimes high, sometimes low. However, the annual estimates have not only been high in each year since the inception of the system, but the overestimates have been substantial, amounting to $333 billion from 1984 to 1994, an average of $30.3 billion per year. Part of these overestimates of liabilities should have been returned to DoD in the form of reduced future accrual payments, but no actuarial mechanism is present to make this return. The result is that DoD payments that amounted to $165 billion between 1984 and 1994 would have been reduced by approximately $30-$40 billion had such an actuarial mechanism been in place, and future scheduled payments would have been reduced significantly more.

Finally, management incentives are significantly weakened by the uncertainty associated with fungibility of accrual funds. While DoD has recovered a portion of accrual savings for real spending authority, the process is uncertain and the recovered amounts have been treated as discretionary spending for OSD rather than returned to the services.

Our recommendations include some directed toward improving the accuracy, timeliness, and availability of accrual estimates, and making changes that would have decisionmakers in each service bear more directly the results of personnel decisions. In the former category, we recommend cohort-specific accounting methods, separate NCPs by service and type of personnel, better methods for setting economic and other assumptions, and broadening the Board of Actuaries to include military labor economists to support more-sophisticated methods of setting assumptions. To bring consequences closer to service decisionmakers, we recommend returning accrual gains and losses to DoD through a new side account, service-specific NCPs for officer and enlisted personnel, and movement toward an advance-funding system. Over the past five years, the Board of Actuaries has recommended many of these changes, but inaction by Congress leaves the current method largely unchanged.

APPENDIX

SAMPLE CALCULATION OF NORMAL COST PERCENTAGE

ACTUAL YEAR-OF-ENTRY (YOE) COHORT-SPECIFIC NCPs

Table A.1 shows the officer and enlisted input vectors for cohorts entering in FY70, FY75, FY80, and FY85.[1] These vectors are actual data for years up to FY90 (e.g., YOS1 only for the 1990 cohort, but YOS1 through YOS20 data are accurate for the 1970 cohort). Future data are projected using recent experience to estimate the necessary continuation rates. In this case, average decrement rates for FY87-89 are used to project future inventories. The cumulative cohort decrement rates for officer and enlisted personnel are shown in Figures A.1 and A.2, and compared with the synthetic cohort rates.

An NCP can be calculated for every YOE cohort that has personnel remaining on active duty. The calculations proceed essentially as occurred for those using synthetic cohorts. The differences are that actual payoffs can be used for past years for each cohort, as can actual interest rates. Thus, instead of calculating the projected future pay of a synthetic new-entry cohort, we calculate the total pay of each actual new-entry cohort by using actual data where available and make projections only where required. Future retirement benefits are calculated essentially as they were for synthetic cohorts, with the retirement category being determined by the entry date. We also use the same future economic assumptions as used in the synthetic cohort.

The cohort-specific NCPs for the selected years are shown in Table A.2, and are compared to the values calculated by the synthetic-cohort method. The synthetic-cohort NCPs correspond to the particular benefit category for the cohort (e.g., the FY70, FY75, and FY80 cohorts are FP,

---

[1]The vectors represent actual historical data and thus are not scaled to an entering cohort of 100,000 as was the synthetic cohort. However, normal cost percentage (NCP) calculations are insensitive to scaling factors because both the numerator (liabilities) and denominator (payroll) depend directly on the number of entering individuals.

Table A.1

Input to the NCP: Cohort Model

	Active-Duty Personnel										
	Officer						Enlisted				
YOE	1970	1975	1980	1985	1990	YOE	1970	1975	1980	1985	1990
YOS						YOS					
1	38707	17739	18188	19683	17777	1	583905	369409	325394	271072	230678
2	46457	18959	19969	21444	21766	2	484025	301964	289910	250166	206863
3	28739	15501	19667	21221	22035	3	211925	250694	254800	221109	180462
4	23044	14234	18504	19613	20723	4	153318	176044	184648	169809	144428
5	18212	13266	16862	17879	18770	5	69077	95273	117829	110632	97721
6	15744	12337	15737	17125	17377	6	62472	80284	101891	95995	85429
7	14026	11439	14554	16101	16322	7	53875	66568	86130	81090	71354
8	13110	11090	13166	14637	14835	8	47132	60056	77125	71932	63142
9	12184	10964	12181	13575	13765	9	39425	54324	66603	63587	55488
10	11516	10890	11577	12954	13139	10	34974	49546	60952	57834	50188
11	11384	10824	11583	12520	12704	11	32052	45678	54548	52464	45151
12	11242	10581	10795	11639	11810	12	30446	42839	50936	49006	41879
13	11240	9993	10480	11275	11431	13	29307	40562	47939	46117	39214
14	11124	9885	10335	11106	11248	14	27789	38430	45540	43802	37082
15	11044	9861	10328	11082	11219	15	26719	37092	43815	42151	35530
16	10774	10147	10259	11001	11133	16	26014	35380	42465	40860	34379
17	10719	10094	10202	10933	11064	17	25414	34493	41415	39855	33482
18	10643	10067	10173	10895	11023	18	25009	33801	40604	39080	32784
19	10613	10043	10148	10862	10989	19	24644	33300	40018	38517	32291
20	11357	9965	10068	10779	10905	20	24303	32734	39356	37906	31698
21	6691	5676	5732	6140	6208	21	13020	10883	13138	12618	10559
22	5261	4471	4510	4828	4880	22	9041	7562	9184	8818	7345
23	4486	3809	3843	4118	4158	23	6743	5623	6853	6594	5441
24	3917	3326	3355	3595	3630	24	5087	4240	5171	4982	4101
25	3376	2869	2893	3100	3128	25	3950	3297	4047	3901	3198
26	2943	2501	2521	2702	2725	26	3341	2781	3419	3301	2688
27	2430	2066	2083	2231	2250	27	2222	1861	2265	2188	1815
28	1994	1696	1710	1831	1846	28	1552	1304	1592	1536	1278
29	1558	1328	1337	1431	1441	29	1053	890	1075	1038	879
30	1258	1074	1080	1156	1163	30	782	661	799	773	653
31	1777	1523	1521	1628	1638	31	269	208	255	248	210

the FY85 is HI-3, and FY90 is REDUX). The actual cohort method shows significantly lower NCPs than does the synthetic cohort method for all years except FY90. These differences result from the use of actual historical data, rather than the synthetic decrement rates and current economic assumptions.

Interestingly, the two NCP calculations show divergent trends. The synthetic-cohort NCPs decrease, while the actual-cohort-method NCPs increase. The decreasing trend of the synthetic cohort is attributable

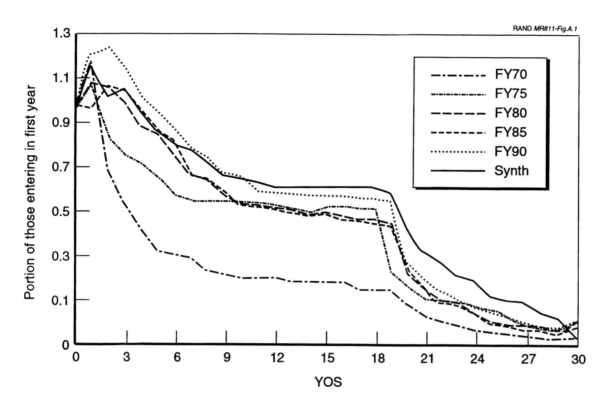

Figure A.1--Cumulative Cohort Decrement Rates--Officer

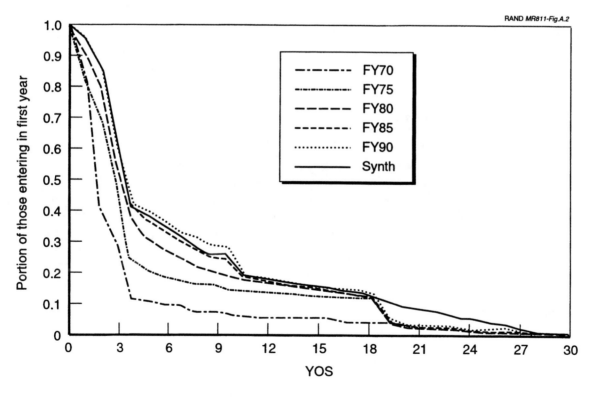

Figure A.2--Cumulative Cohort Decrement Rates--Enlisted

Table A.2

NCP Output-Cohort Model

Year of Entry	1970	1975	1980	1985	1990
Present value of future basic pay ($000)	10,708,936	11,686,028	16,111,843	21,892,440	25,105,577
Present value of future benefits ($000)	2,387,675	3,602,515	5,857,785	8,552,572	8,872,259
Normal cost percentage	22.3%	30.8%	36.4%	39.1%	35.3%
Valuation report	49.4%	49.4%	49.4%	43.4%	36.6%

to the declining level of retirement benefits for more recent cohorts. The actual cohort data takes into account this declining benefit structure, as well as the increasing trends in continuation rates and the changing payroll and interest trends. These calculations show that when all factors affecting NCPs are considered, retirement costs are increasing rather than decreasing in the DoD. *From a management perspective, the synthetic-cohort method provides a misleading trend in retirement costs.*

DoD Annual Accrual Payments

The annual DoD accrual payment is computed from year-of-entry cohort NCPs in the same manner as used to obtain the accrual payment from the benefit-specific cohorts obtained in the synthetic cohort calculations in Section 2. The specific procedure is shown in Table A.3. The percentage of the annual payroll earmarked for personnel in each corresponding year of service is shown in the second column, while the NCP pertaining to that year group is shown in the third column. The weighted average required for the appropriate NCP is then obtained by multiplying corresponding components of those two columns and summing the resulting products. The overall NCP of 0.349 resulting from this procedure is then multiplied by the FY90 military basic payroll to obtain DoD's retirement accrual payment for the FY90 federal budget. This NCP is lower than the corresponding NCP of 0.438, which is the

Table A.3

Actual-Cohort NCPs

Year of Service	% of FY90 Basic Payroll	NCP Applied
1	7.5	0.353
2	7.6	0.347
3	6.9	0.343
4	5.6	0.341
5	5.2	0.397
6	5.4	0.391
7	4.8	0.374
8	4.5	0.369
9	4.2	0.360
10	4.1	0.339
11	4.0	0.364
12	3.9	0.377
13	3.9	0.374
14	3.9	0.346
15	3.7	0.322
16	3.5	0.308
17	3.4	0.302
18	3.5	0.281
19	3.6	0.279
20	2.8	0.263
21	1.7	0.223
22	1.3	0.204
23	1.2	0.214
24	1.0	0.202[a]
25	0.8	0.202
26	0.6	0.202
27	0.5	0.202
28	0.4	0.202
29	0.3	0.202
30+	0.2	0.202
FY90 Weighted Value		0.335
Valuation Report		0.438

[a]We have data beginning with the FY67 cohort. We have used this NCP for earlier entering cohorts.

synthetic-cohort value for FY90 obtained in the 1989 evaluation report. The lower NCP results from increased accuracy from use of historical data.

REFERENCES

Asch, Beth J., and J. Warner, *A Theory of Military Compensation and Personnel Policy*, MR-439-OSD, Santa Monica, Calif.: RAND, 1994a.

Asch, Beth J., and J. Warner, *A Policy Analysis of Alternate Military Retirement Systems*, MR-465-OSD, Santa Monica, Calif.: RAND, 1994b.

Chapter 74, Title 10, United States Code (which incorporates the original legislation from Public Law 98-94).

Department of Defense Authorization Act, 1984, Report of the Committee on Armed Services, Report No. 98-107, 98th Congress, House of Representatives, Section 1053, "Accrual Funding for the Military Retirement System," May 11, 1983.

Department of Defense, Retirement Board of Actuaries, Report to the President and Congress on the Status of the Department of Defense Military Retirement Fund, December 31, 1992.

Department of Defense, Office of the Actuary, *Valuation of the Military Retirement System*, September 30, 1986.

Department of Defense, Office of the Actuary, *Valuation of the Military Retirement System*, September 30, 1987.

Department of Defense, Office of the Actuary, *Valuation of the Military Retirement System*, September 30, 1988.

Department of Defense, Office of the Actuary, *Valuation of the Military Retirement System*, September 30, 1989.

Department of Defense, Office of the Actuary, *Valuation of the Military Retirement System*, September 30, 1990.

Department of Defense, Office of the Actuary, *Valuation of the Military Retirement System*, September 30, 1991.

Department of Defense, Office of the Actuary, *Valuation of the Military Retirement System*, September 30, 1992.

Department of Defense, Office of the Actuary, *Valuation of the Military Retirement System*, September 30, 1993.

Department of Defense, Office of the Actuary, *Valuation of the Military Retirement System*, September 30, 1994.

Department of Defense, Office of the Actuary, *Valuation of the Military Retirement System*, September 30, 1995.

Department of Defense, Office of the Actuary, *Valuation of the Military Retirement System*, September 30, 1996.

Grady, John H., Sam Gutterman, Kathleen P. Utgoff, and Carolyn Weaver, *Panel Report on RAND Recommendations for Changes in the Calculation of Accrual Payments to Fund Military Retirement*, Washington, D.C.: Law Offices of Groom and Nordberg, April 23, 1992 (unpublished).

Grissmer, David W., Richard L. Eisenman, and William W. Taylor, *Defense Downsizing: An Evaluation of Alternative Voluntary Separation Payments to Military Personnel*, Santa Monica, Calif.: RAND, MR-171-OSD/A, 1995.

Hix, W. M., and W. W. Taylor, *A Policymaker's Guide to Accrual Funding of Military Retirement*, MR-760-A, Santa Monica, Calif.: RAND, 1997.

Kirby, S. N., and H. Thie, *Enlisted Personnel Management, A Historical Perspective*, MR-755-OSD, Santa Monica, Calif: RAND, 1996.

Thie, H., and R. A. Brown, *Future Career Management Systems for U.S. Military Officers*, MR-470-OSD, Santa Monica CA: RAND, 1994.